2021

Natalie

You are a Blessing to
the world!

Keep smiling

Susan

Creating Life Balance

CREATING
LIFE
BALANCE

Strategies to Thrive

CREATING LIFE BALANCE

Strategies to Thrive

Susan A. Davis, ThM

Published by Susan A. Davis, ThM
Port Orange, Florida

First Edition, October 2020
ISBN: 978-1-7356476-0-9 ebook
ISBN: 978-1-7356476-1-6 paperback

Library of Congress Cataloging-in-Publication Data
Davis, Susan, 2020- Creating Life Balance: Strategies to Thrive
Published by Susan A. Davis

Library of Congress Control Number: 2020917151

Editor: Regina Huber
www.TransformYourPerformance.com

Cover Design & Layout:
Julie A. Davis Veach
www.JulieDavisVeach.com

Author Photo: Collete Davis, Julie A. Davis Veach

♥

Dedicated to all my family and friends
who continue to love and support me.

Creating Life Balance

Optimizing Performance in the Workplace & Life

Mindfulness training is a unique self-actualization method that empowers participants to fully engage all facets of life.

Mindfulness training has also been called attention training, resiliency training, brain training and situational awareness training.

And some state the term should be re-coined, as it doesn't express what it is really about: being present, able to maintain a state of emotional balance that allows us to be fully functional and lead a happier life at the same time.

Contents

DISCLAIMER

These suggestions and practices are an important addition to both holistic and traditional medical treatment programs. Please use this information in conjunction with the advice of your physician or healthcare practitioner.

Foreword

By Matt Maurer, Founder and COO of Stroll Inc.

Even long before Shark Tank was popular on TV, many of you probably had a fantasy even above other career-based fantasies to manifest that great idea…to start a company and take your rightful place among the entrepreneurial elite. We all know someone, who knows someone who did it overnight, and now owns a giant penthouse in downtown [insert preferred major city]. But as a card-carrying member of the company-creating class, let me be probably-not-the-first to tell you it is no smooth road. For 99.77% of us that try, it is as difficult and dimly-lit a road as any you will venture down in your life – the lows are as low as the highs are high, and one way or another you will crash into, fall onto, or have dropped upon you, a giant. brick. wall.

This can be generally true of life, but it's easier to describe within the context of trying to do something big and chaotic. Whether you find yourself near that crash point now, or you're lucky and you simply recognize that you someday might, there are things you can do – real, practical, tactical moves you can make ahead of time to shield yourself for when that existential enemy shows up at your door. Because the first casualty will be your most important asset – you! Your health is what powers your general capacity for action. And it is your health, all angles of it, that will be stolen during your biggest challenges, and it's the mark of someone willing to put in the work, to play the long game, to definitively understand this reality and put a strategy to work now so that they don't have to inevitably realize the need for reassessment later.

And so, thank goodness for this book, and for Susan, who has not only studied many lifetimes of material across a dozen or more human institutions, but has decades of experience practically applying what she's learned in some of the most challenging and tragic of human situations. She has distilled that experience down into first principles and practices that you can weave into your life today or fill your quiver with for to beat stress at its own game.

If the advice sounds simple, it is only because Susan has—in the vein of Oliver Wendell Holmes—arrived at the simplicity which exists "on the other side of complexity", which I think is the best any author can offer, all the more valuable if you're someone who's only interested in the cliff notes because there is too much work to be done. To that I say absorb what you can, familiarize with the principles, keep this reference nearby, and get back to work.

Author's Preface

The human brain hasn't changed very much in thousands of years, but the world around it sure has. Sometimes it is hard to keep up with the rapid advances in technology and the breakneck pace of everyday living. People are actively looking for tools to help them cope with techno stress. This book offers multiple practices that will fit in to your lifestyle.

As a successful, or soon-to-be successful, business owner, you may have wondered, "How can I possibly keep up this pace?"

The purpose of this book is to REIGNITE YOUR FLAME AND PREVENT GETTING BURNT OUT TO KEEP YOU AT THE TOP OF YOUR GAME.

I can help you achieve your goals, reaching your full potential through assessment, self-awareness, action and sustainment. This book is a resource to help you regain your balance!

With acute awareness and mindfulness, optimizing performance in the workplace and life will become a simple practice. Building strong leaders, creating balance between work and home-life, developing personal power through self-awareness and improving attention and concentration will enable you to make better overall decisions.

Top leaders in every organization are taking a hard look at what mindfulness training can do for them. Elite athletes, educators, the entertainment industry, as well as entrepreneurs are finding relief and surprising positive outcomes, as they begin to implement a few simple strategies.

Mindfulness training not only alleviates stress and anxiety, but also reduces depression and improves immune system function and cognitive skills.

When the thinking brain (prefrontal cortex) and the emotional brain (limbic systems, particularly the amygdala) work well together, we are in a state of calm, rational and thoughtful behavior. When these two hemispheres are not in balance, we feel stressed, angry and vulnerable. Neuroplasticity, is the brain's ability to change in response to experience and training. Neuroplasticity is where the neural synapses and pathways are altered as an effect of behavioral, environmental and neural changes. The more awareness we have to that which we do not want, the more control we have of making lasting changes.

I will introduce to you my cure for today's burnt out communities, -the Basic Recipe-as I call it; to fine tune your Biology. This includes Oxygen, Water, Magnesium and Movement.

Functional Medicine

In addition to the Personal Stress Assessment, you may also want to investigate your medical system. Your future may depend on your understanding of your biology.

Conventional medicine practitioners do not add in other practices to their acute care mode. In other words, they do not look at the root cause of their patient's issue whereas, complementary medicine is patient centered, looking at nourishment, environment and breaking down barriers that contribute to imbalance.

Conventional medicine is aligned with scientific studies that are mostly funded by the pharmaceutical industry. Anything outside this established framework would be described as integrative, complementary, alternative, traditional or functional medicine. (Boon, NG, Thompson & Whitehead, 2016)

Integrative medicine (IM) health care is an approach using multiple aspects to improve the quality of life of an individual, including emotional, spiritual, mental and social approaches sometimes including traditional medicine based on culture.

Functional Medicine (FM) focuses on the patient rather than the disease and is more aligned with naturopathic medicine. This system looks at the biology, gene environment, organ health and biochemistry of an individual.

FM has taken the somatic hypochondriasis to find the root case. Under this system the patient has a review of organ systems, cellular etiology, environment, diet and lifestyle.

The body will function optimally when given the right conditions; the goal for each person is to achieve optimal organ and body function. FM is "focused on defining individual function/dysfunction and less on the lumping of individuals into specific disease categories." (Bland, 2017)

- Interprets labs differently

- Run more extensive labs

- Customized health care

- Spends more 1-1 time with patients

- Addresses underlying dysfunctions

- Does not shy away from natural treatments

Some common conditions that are treated are ADHD, GERD, digestive complaints, irritable bowel syndrome, ulcerative colitis, Crohn's disease, thyroid dysfunction, hormonal imbalance, depression/anxiety, diabetes/prediabetes, psoriasis, auto-immune conditions, preconception planning, allergies and Lyme disease.

"Aetna Insurance reported a decrease of $2,000 annually in healthcare costs as well as an estimated $3,000 increase in productivity for employees training in mindfulness."

The Atlantic, Pinsker

"As I'm talking with people about finding meaningful work, I'm finding that there are 2 steps. The first step is the exercise in getting clarity on what you want to do. The second is identifying opportunities and pursuing them."

Tommy Leep

Introduction

Are you prepared for success?

Do you think you deserve it?

If you are carrying unconscious beliefs (keyword = unconscious), which are keeping you from realizing your greatest dreams, wouldn't you want to know what they are and how best to address them?

The two main characteristics that stand out to me with entrepreneurs are PASSION & DRIVE. But what happens when burnout gives way to exhaustion and a lack of clarity, or worse, unhappiness? How do you regain balance and joy?

The question to ask yourself is, "How do I learn to use my mind in an entirely different way and yet still keep my edge?" Am I productive or just busy?

In this book we will explore the correlation between our everyday thoughts and behaviors to what is known as "frequency" or positive vibes. When we are sad, tired, frustrated or angry, our frequency is low. However, when we are happy and feel optimistic, our frequency is high.

Creating a high frequency for longer periods of time also eventually translates into actual physical manifestation! Like creates like, this is the law of attraction. What are you creating?

Entrepreneurs are usually trying to exercise more control over their time. As entrepreneurs, we have the luxury of structuring our workday in a way that best suits us. How will we choose to make each moment beneficial for both our body and mind?

Together we can remove and eliminate both the conscious and unconscious behaviors, which are keeping you from attaining your goals.

Remember- the best ideas are manifested when we are aware of our total well being. You will get more done by working fewer hours. Step away-just for a moment. This is an opportunity to pay attention to your body, to recalibrate and become balanced. This is the true key to success!

When I am teaching and training in Silicon Valley and NYC, I notice many of those in attendance are not "with me." I refer to this as having too many tabs open on your hard drive. My purpose is to help each individual start to delete those tabs that are not necessarily contributing to the forward motion of the project.

A question to ask might be, "How can I increase my focus without losing my edge? Am I busy or productive?"

It's essential that we become aware of what we need to be a balanced entrepreneur. This includes our biology... increased oxygen and water, as well as magnesium in the form of sea salts or Epsom salts, for soaking. If we are to maintain momentum, achieve success, make that pitch and secure those funds, balancing work and play will soon become a priority. A Balanced Entrepreneur will contribute positively to all attributes of your business.

This book is written to help individuals to improve their businesses, relationships, performance and overall well-being.

The unique factor within these pages is the physical 'take-aways' you will discover, that are simple and applicable in real time.

According to Dr. Norm Shealy, "all known diseases are deficient in Oxygen, Water and Magnesium." If you want to be successful in all aspects of your life, your relationships, career and finances, awareness of these elements is a must.

Do you currently feel anxious, depressed or in pain? Would you like to quit smoking? Increase your productivity? Change the way you relate to others? Do you want to change your world? This training can help you get your life back.

The tools in this book will help you:

- Restore self-confidence
- Assist with key goals
- Increase creativity
- Help manage change during periods of growth
- Boost productivity and effectiveness
- Develop strong communication skills
- Help attract and retain the best and brightest employees
- Bring work-life balance back into the lives of employees
- Help your employees to grow and thrive

Take-Away

The unique factor within these pages is the physical 'takeaways', which you will discover are simple and applicable in real time! Most chapters will end with some concrete practices that you can choose, one or a few that you are most drawn to, and begin to incorporate them into your own world. I don't expect you to do all of them, that is why there are several to choose from. This book is written to help individuals improve their business, relationships, performance and well-being. There are a couple of meditations or home scripts for you to read at your leisure to help you hit the ground running. The key to high performance is reducing stress, anxiety and depression while improving the immune system and cognitive skills.

Now that we have discovered, or rediscovered, some of the benefits of mindfulness, let's look at what actionable steps can be taken to change our lives for the better.

I remember when I first took the Personal Stress Assessment Test. I thought that stress was "normal", but what I didn't realize is that it actually isn't! The following assessment tool is to help identify the stressors in your personal life. Once we have them identified we can begin to reduce and eliminate these stressors with the simple practices and strategies suggested in the following pages.

Take a moment to fill out the Personal Stress Assessment - Total Life Stress Test by Norman Shealy, PhD, MD, Neurosurgeon with author's permission.

LET'S GET STARTED!

Your choices will change the world.

95% of our behavior is determined by our unconscious mind or program.

We can intentionally change our brains with training.

Personal Stress Assessment

PART A: Dietary Stress

AVERAGE DAILY SUGAR CONSUMPTION

Sugar added to food or drink	1 point per 5 teaspoons	
Sweet roll, piece of pie/cake, brownie, or other desert	1 point each	
Coke or can of pop, candy bar	2 points each	
Banana split, commercial milk shake, sundae, etc.	5 points each	
White flour (white bread, spaghetti, etc.)	5 points	

AVERAGE DAILY SALT CONSUMPTION

Little or no "added" salt	0 points	
Few salty foods (pretzels, potato chips, etc.)	0 points	
Moderate "added" salt and/or salty foods at least once per day	3 points	
Heavy salt user, regularly (user of "table salt" and/or salty foods at least twice a day).	10 points	

AVERAGE DAILY CAFFEINE CONSUMPTION

Coffee	½ point/cup	
Tea	½ point/cup	
Cola drink or Soda	1 point/cup	
2 Anacin or Aspirin tablets	½ point/dose	
Caffeine Benzoate tablets	2 points each	

AVERAGE WEEKLY EATING OUT

2-4 times per week	3 points	
5-10 times per week	6 points	
More than 10 times per week	10 points	

DIETARY SUBTOTAL

DIETARY SUBTOTAL	

PART B: Environmental Stress

DRINKING WATER

Chlorinated only	1 point	
Chlorinated and fluoridated	2 points	

SOIL & AIR POLLUTION

Live within 10 miles of city of 500,000 or more	10 points	
Live within 10 miles of city of 250,000 or more	5 points	
Live within 10 miles of city of 50,000 or more	2 points	
Live in the country but use pesticides, herbicides and/or chemical fertilizer	10 points	
Exposed to cigarette smoke of someone else more than 1 hour per day	5 points	

Creating Life Balance

TELEVISION WATCHED		
For each hour over 1 per day	½ point	
ENVIRONMENTAL SUBTOTAL		

PART C: Chemical Stress

DRUGS (ANY AMOUNT OF USAGE)		
Antidepressants	1 point	
Tranquilizers	3 points	
Sleeping pills	3 points	
Narcotics	3 points	
Other pain relievers	3 points	
Nicotine		
3-10 cigarettes per day	5 points	
11-20 cigarettes per day	15 points	
21-30 cigarettes per day	20 points	
31-40 cigarettes per day	40 points	
Over 40 cigarettes per day	1 point each	
Cigar (s)	1 point each	
Pipeful(s)	1 point each	
Chewing tobacco – "chews" per day	1 point each	

AVERAGE DAILY ALCOHOL CONSUMPTION		
1 oz. Whiskey, gin, vodka, etc.	2 points each	
8 oz. Beer	2 points each	
4-6 oz. Glass of wine	2 points each	
CHEMICAL SUBTOTAL		

PART D: Physical Stress

WEIGHT		
Underweight more than 10 pounds	5 points	
10 to 15 lbs. Overweight	5 points	
16 to 25 lbs. Overweight	10 points	
26-40 lbs. Overweight	25 points	
More than 40 lbs. Overweight	40 points	

ACTIVITY

Adequate exercise *, 3 days or more per week	0 points	
Some physical exercise 1 or 2 days per week	15 points	
No regular exercise	40 points	

*Adequate means doubling heartbeat and/or sweating minimum of 30 minutes per time

WORK

Sit most of the day	3 points	
Industrial/factory worker	3 points	
Overnight travel more than once a week	5 points	
Work more than 50 hours per week	2 points per hour over 50	
Work varying shifts	10 points	
Work night shifts	5 points	

PHYSICAL SUBTOTAL

PART E: Emotional Stress

SLEEP

Less than 7 hours per night	3 points	
Usually 7 or 8 hours per night	0 points	
More than 8 hours per night	2 points	

RELAXATION

Relax only during sleep	10 points	
Relax or meditate at least 20 minutes per day	0 points	

FRUSTRATION AT WORK

Enjoy work	0 points	
Mildly frustrated by job	1 point	
Moderately frustrated by job	3 points	
Very frustrated by job	5 points	

MARITAL STATUS		
Married, happily	0 points	
Married, moderately unhappy	2 points	
Married, very unhappy	5 points	
Unmarried man over 30	5 points	
Unmarried woman over 30	2 points	
USUAL MOOD		
Happy, well adjusted	0 points	
Moderately angry, depressed or frustrated	10 points	
Very angry, depressed or frustrated	20 points	
ANY OTHER MAJOR STRESS NOT MENTIONED ABOVE YOU JUDGE INTENSITY (SPECIFY):		
10-40 points		
EMOTIONAL SUBTOTAL		

PART F: Homes-Rahe Social Readjustment Rating*

Circle the mean values that correspond with life events listed below which you have experienced during the past 12 months.

*The Social Readjustment Rating Scale: See Homes, T.H. & Rahe, R.H.: The social readjustment rating scale. Journal of Psychosomatic Research. 11:213-218, 1967, for complete wording of these items.

Death of a spouse	100	
Divorce	73	
Marital Separation	65	
Jail term	63	
Death of a close family member	63	
Personal injury or illness	53	
Marriage	50	
Fired at work	47	
Marital reconciliation	45	
Retirement	45	
Change in health of family member	44	
Pregnancy	40	
Sexual difficulties	39	
Gain of new family member	39	
Business readjustment	39	
Change in financial state	38	

Death of close friend	37	
Change to different line of work	36	
Change in number of arguments with spouse	35	
Mortgage over $20,000	31	
Foreclosure or mortgage or loan	30	
Change in responsibilities at work	29	
Son or daughter leaving home	29	
Trouble with in-laws	29	
Outstanding personal achievement	28	
Spouse begin or stop work	26	
Begin or end school	25	
Change in living conditions	24	
Revision of personal habits	23	
Trouble with boss	20	
Change in work hour or conditions	20	
Change in residence	20	
Change in schools	19	
Change in recreation	19	
Change in church activities	18	
Change in social activities	17	
Mortgage or loan less than $20,000	16	
Change in sleeping habits	15	
Change in eating habits	15	
Vacation, especially if away from home	13	
Christmas, or other major holiday stress	12	
Minor violation of the law	11	

Add the mean values to get the Holmes-Rahe total.

Then refer to the conversion table on the next page, to determine your number of points.

If points are greater than 200, then you run a very great risk of a major accident or illness within 1 year.

YOUR NUMBER OF POINTS	HOLMES-RAHE LESS THAN
0	60
1	110
2	160
3	170
4	180
5	190
6	200
7	210
8	220
9	230
10	240
11	250
12	260
13	265
14	270
15	275
16	280
17	285
18	290
19	295
20	300
21	305
22	310
23	315
24	320
25	325
26	330
27	335
28	340
29	345
ANYTHING OVER 351 = 40+	

ADD SECTIONS A-F TOGETHER

A +	
B +	
C +	
D +	
E +	
F	
Total	

Personal Stress Assessment Score

If your score exceeds 25 points, you probably will feel better if you reduce your stress; greater than 50 points, you definitely need to eliminate stress in your life.

Circle your stressor with the highest number of points and work first to eliminate it; then circle your next greatest stressor, overcome it; and so on.

27

Why Now?

Your mind is a browser of reality, and you have too many tabs open. Are we relying on technology to take on the function of our memory? For example, most of us now rely on GPS to navigate everywhere, and we no longer know how to get anywhere without it! For myself, I have stopped memorizing phone numbers because I just hit call or ask Siri to dial it for me.

Having our phone within reach 24/7 may not be in our best interest biologically and emotionally. Just like our devices we need to power down and reboot! In this fast-paced society, keeping up with the newest technology, online dating, Facebook, Twitter, Instagram, Linked-In, etc..., and concern about our age and our future family can be strenuous.

People don't have the time to work at work. Between blinking chat apps, overflowing inboxes and relentless meetings, who has the time to be productive? Because of this, the workday runs over into evenings and weekends. In this age of constant information and ability to access entertainment, the most important relationship to us is in peril. This is the relationship with ourselves.

When you are physically, emotionally and mentally stressed this can soon become chronic. And burnout sets in. Are you feeling like nothing is working out for you? Do you continue to feel like your list of things to get done is getting longer and longer? Burnout can creep into your life; it doesn't happen all at once. We have come to believe that we have to put up with this, but we don't. It may have become the norm (condition), but that doesn't mean we have to follow this unhealthy norm.

All of this contributes to holding our breath. What happens when we unconsciously hold our breath? We begin to suffer from lack of oxygen and a build-up of carbon dioxide. Breathing is voluntary and involuntary. The medulla oblongata and the pons carolli are the respiratory centers of our brain. These centers of our brain are stimulated by the carbon dioxide content of the blood- the more carbon dioxide in the blood the faster the breathing. We are now headed into the flight-or-fight response: our heart beats faster, blood pressure shoots up and our breathing quickens. This is that feeling of "I need to get out of here."

Let's talk about water. Our body is approximately 60% water. When we do not have enough water in our body the neurotransmitters and functioning cells cannot communicate optimally, thus, creating more sleeplessness, anxiety, pain and even depression.

Are these fitness apps really working?

They may be working but are we responding to the prompts in a good way?

I mean if we put in 10,000 steps what does that really mean to my spine, lungs and heart?

Movement with intention is just that, intending to increase lung capacity, intending to strengthen our spine, lower back and respiratory system.

Do we really know why we can't sleep or why our relationships are falling apart?

This is the opportunity to begin to recognize what your stress looks like and how you can reverse it.

"I have a better idea:

Die young–at a very old age."

Steven R. Gundry
The Plant Paradox

"Today's leadership needs to unlearn outdated approaches and legacy behaviors that impede progress and embrace a new skill set, tool-set, and mindset that can inspire and empower both the individual and the organization to adapt and evolve."

Corporate Innovation at Singularity University

I was introduced to Kym McNicholas by my granddaughter, Collete Davis. Together they had just finished a successful experiential project at the racetrack for entrepreneurs. She is a vivacious, articulate journalist, enjoy her story.

Kym's Story

In 2007 I was the morning anchor for a local television news program and part of my job I learned was to emcee community events. The irony was that I got into television because I never felt comfortable sharing my voice with people in person. I was so shy that I used to sit in the dark room during lunch in high school. It wasn't until I got into college and my mom telling the dean of the communications department that I needed to take some communications courses, that I learned the power of the microphone. While experiencing intense anxiety to talk in front of groups of friends or even a class to deliver a project presentation, I didn't struggle with talking to the camera or into a microphone. Suddenly judgments seemed far away if not non-existent.

After doing my first community event, I walked into my general manager's office and quit because I didn't feel I could do the job any longer. The screen did not protect me, and my anxiety came back with a vengeance. But I'm not the type to just rest on my laurels and totally give up. I realized I had the ability to talk to people through the camera... I just needed to learn how to remove the camera. So, I threw myself into the fire and took a minimum wage job announcing the dolphin show at Six Flags in front of hundreds of people a day. I had to do it. It was my job. They put you on stage and you would just have to perform, unlike the dolphins that were not forced to perform. They only performed if they chose to and if they chose to, they would get a treat. So, I got a lot of experience ad-libbing and filling time. How in the world did I do this? I pretended I was Britney Spears. If I was Britney Spears, people would just love me anyway. All I would have to do is just walk on stage and if I was Britney Spears, people would cheer no matter what.

The power of imagination. That's what got me to nail every show!!

However, as I progressed in my career and started working at Forbes Magazine, speaking on panels, giving keynote presentations, and more, I started feeling less and less authentic. Although, all of the information I was presenting was 100% what I intended, I felt like an impostor. Going up on stage and in my mind pretending I was someone else in order to speak my truth, didn't feel right anymore. I would have to have my Forbes videographer come to my events to give me real feedback as to how I did on stage, because I was feeling so crummy inside. I remember one event in particular where I was interviewing two well-renowned authors Carmine Gallo and Carol Goman. I was really under-the-weather that evening, with a stuffed-up nose, sore throat, and throbbing migraine. I couldn't even tell you what I asked the two guests or the insight I provided to the audience during our presentation. All I remember was thinking, "Britney Spears" before I went on stage. It was habit by that point. But afterwards, I was really down on myself and yet, people walked up to me and said that was one of the best Churchill Club events they'd ever been to because of my moderating skills. It would happen at just about every event where people would say, "Wow you were the best speaker I've ever heard on this topic," and I would think in my head every single time, "Were we in the same room?" But my videographer would set me straight and affirm what others would say.

If I was so good at speaking in front of people, then why did I always feel so bad? Why was I still scared to death and have almost debilitating anxiety attacks before every single presentation? I couldn't figure it out. Then I met "Mimi." Her granddaughter, Collete Davis, was a friend of mine. I was introduced to Collete because a mutual colleague asked me to help Collete attain media skills and introductions to local press as she was going to be a famous professional race car driver. Collete had not been in a race car in years. But when she was, she topped the charts. She knew that's what she wanted. She knew it's who she was in her heart of hearts. So, even though Collete wasn't in a car now, she believed with all of who she was that she "IS" a professional race car driver. This girl and her sense of self, authenticity, purity, groundedness, and unmatching confidence blew me away. I believed, because she did that, she was able to create who she said she wanted to be. And I couldn't help but think, how in the world does someone get these wonderful traits! How could I do the same? How could I believe with my whole heart who I am. How could I get rid of that feeling of being an impostor on stage but in social situations as well, where I felt intense anxiety because of caring so much about what other people think. So, Collete introduced me to Mimi.

Mimi is Collete's grandmother and played a large role in raising her. She and I connected right away on an amazingly high level. She offered me a few breathing exercises, one which was counterintuitive to what I'd previously been told by experts. She said when you get anxiety; you sometimes are breathing in too fast. So, breathe in for fewer counts and deepen your breath and then breathe out slower. Everyone else would tell me to breathe in more counts, which actually made it worse, I was actually hyperventilating! Her reversal of the way I breathe truly had an impact on me. The other tip she gave me, especially in social situations, was to simply place my hand over my heart when I needed to feel grounded. She taught me how to do it in the most inconspicuous manner so no one would be alarmed by my action. Actually, in many situations it comes across as endearing, and engaging, and heartfelt to others, inviting them in non-verbal manner to feel more comfortable to open up more. In fact, I've used that technique on stage and on camera in numerous situations where I felt like even the other person on stage was anxious. One such situation was at a Girls In Tech Catalyst Conference where I was the emcee. During lunch, we had a few young women in the audience hanging out. So, I thought, "Why not showcase another inspiring woman for a few minutes?" So, I pulled a graphic artist who had been bringing life to the speakers the entire event in large murals on the wall on the far side of the room. I asked her to come on stage having no idea that she preferred being in the shadows. When she sat down next to me, she almost burst into tears. That's when I put my arm across my chest and hand over my heart and look at her with a big smile and then looked at the audience and spoke my truth about why I thought this woman was so inspiring to me. As I spoke, she began to relax a bit and was able to answer some incredibly heartfelt questions. So, it was a trick that not only helps ground myself, but also helps to ground others.

I couldn't believe two simple tips could have such an impact on my life. So, I wondered what more Mimi could offer. That's when she offered a resolution session. I was not a big believer in past lives, let alone having them impact who I am today. But there was a little spec of curiosity that led me to try several sessions with her. She said, "Have you ever wondered where some thoughts come from that you can't remember experiences that would've ever led you to know something or do something?" And that got me. I often wondered about my subconscious mind. Sometimes I think a thought or imagine something, and I wonder where that could've come from as it didn't come from a real-life experience. For example, why was I so scared to be on stage and so afraid of talking to people or truly letting them know who I am and even allowing myself to be who I am.

The sessions would always stress me out at first because Mimi would ask me, "What's going through your mind right now?" And honestly it would either seem irrelevant or there would be nothing but darkness. But she urged me to trust the process. And I hesitantly did. And I'm glad I did. At first when we got to a point where I saw myself on a medieval stage long ago as a large

6 foot plus man with a huge mouth wide open, I thought, "What the heck? How is this relevant? Where did this thought come from?" But she urged me to follow it and just let it play out. I feared that I was going to force the thought into some direction. But she assured me it all works out. That your mind always goes in the right direction. So, I kept watching in my mind. And I thought it was odd that this man on stage would have his mouth open and nothing was coming out. Something was wrong. There was someone on the side of that stage that was in a dark outfit that I couldn't make-out. I never figured out who that person was or why they were there. But I knew there was something that was leading to this man on stage to either not be able to speak or sing, or simply not be heard. Yet, people remained calm with their eyes intently on the stage, on that man, who seemed to have no voice. That was about all that played out in my mind as it went to darkness. Then suddenly I saw a little man appear in my mind with a red shiny long robe, and a tall pointy hat. I was thinking in my mind, "Wow, if I believed in fairytales, I would think that was Merlin." I only told Mimi I was seeing a tiny guy in a red shiny robe and pointy hat. She asked, "Is it Merlin?" I can't remember exactly how she put the pieces together for me to this day. I just remember her saying, "It means you do have the magic within you." And I remember her telling me that he was a good sign that I had nothing to fear anymore.

That whatever I may have experienced long ago on that stage in a past life, whether I believe it or not, or wherever that thought had come from, that it would no longer get in my way of not only finding my voice, but speaking my truth confidently and without anxiety.

After that session, my life changed. I went on to emcee an exclusive five-hour event in Silicon Valley where I had to not only introduce the main speakers on stage, but also share my insight. And I didn't find out until 10pm the night before that I had to write all of my own scripts on topics in which I had little familiarity. I didn't get back to my hotel room until 11:30pm and had to be up at 5:30am to head to the venue. You'd think my anxiety would be through the roof. Surprisingly, I was overwhelmed with excitement. With a little bit of research and inspiration from the biographies of the speakers, the words were flowing all night. And even with no sleep, I got up on that stage and flowed my energy, (another trick Mimi had taught me) across the stage throughout the audience. It was such a successful event, that I was approached by someone in the audience whom I was already helping out with ideas for media coverage of his upcoming startup competition, who told me that based on what he saw on that stage that day, he knew I was the right person to not only emcee the semi-finals on stage at the world's largest consumer electronics show in Las Vegas, CES, but also the finals to be held on Necker Island, Virgin's Sir Richard Branson's private island in the British Virgin Islands – where he would also be 'eyes on me' while he judged the competition. What an honor! I couldn't have done that without Mimi.

Ever since then, I've been traveling the world as an emcee for major events including on Capitol Hill in front of more than 200 lawmakers and global tech executives where I was sharing insight on the connected future. I remember when the CEO of Cable Labs, the research and development arm for the entire cable industry, approached me about the event. He said I needed to meet the key person making that decision. Turns out it was former FCC Chairman and current president of the trade association, NCTA (National Cable & Telecommunications Association). He walked right up to me and said he knew exactly who I was and wanted me to not just emcee his event but wanted me to share my perspective on the connected future throughout the entire event. It used to be that I would get so nervous before these events, and now I get excited. After that event, I was exiting stage when a woman approached me. I'll never forget this. She was the co-founder of CNBC and she said, "You were outstanding. I kept wondering if I was going to see more women represented on that stage. But it turns out you were every woman up there. And Maria Barteloromo couldn't have done a better job than you and in fact I was at an event last week where she didn't. You are talented." Yes, that happened. WOW! Thank you, Mimi!

Whether the revelation I had during that life-changing session was truly a past life experience still haunting me today, my subconscious fears manifesting into movies in my mind, or purely my imagination running away from me, it doesn't matter. Mimi's process of getting to the heart of where your greatest fears are coming from, is truly remarkable. Even more, her approach to releasing those fears always down to your DNA, really works. I always think, "How can she top what she's already done?" And she does. Most recently she taught me the most impactful meditation. I have recently been traveling the world as an Executive Storyteller for a company that I discovered as a journalist that was creating the biggest breakthrough in vascular medicine with the potential of tackling the #1 killer in America, Cardiovascular Disease and that it was the same core technology that revolutionized Lasik eye surgery. I also have a show I've been trying to launch about healthcare on KRON 4 TV in San Francisco. On top of that not only did I have to emcee the main annual tech event for one of the largest banks in the world, HSBC, but also several more Girls In Tech Events, and host radio shows, and do interviews for Vator.TV as Editor-In Chief of their Corporate Innovator Series, and, and, and,

and OH MY GOSH! WOULD THE WORLD JUST STOP FOR A MOMENT AND LET ME CATCH-UP!

While I was enjoying every opportunity, I was stressed out beyond belief. I had an amazing session with Mimi where she taught me her latest meditation technique, which literally takes three minutes. I've learned many meditation techniques throughout the years, but none ever succeeded in keeping me faithful as I never really saw long-term results. Well, this one works. It's simply breathing in and saying each breath number out loud for three counts of ten. Simple...But it works. Everything Mimi has offered me works and I owe so much to her coaching!

Kym McNicholas is an Emmy Award-winning Journalist, whose tenure at Forbes led her to becoming the executive director of what's become the world's largest startup competition, the extreme tech challenge, with Sir Richard Branson as the anchor judge. She's since gone on to launch a successful radio show and pod cast, Kym McNicholas on Innovation, has a healthcare show launching on a Bay Area TV station, is a sought-after emcee for events around the world and just helped take Ra Medical Systems public as the Executive Storyteller to the CEO. She is also the Co-Founder of the non-profit organization The Way to My Heart.

Frequency & Positive Vibes

What Is Frequency?

Everything has a frequency! You have a frequency, I have a frequency, and even the chair has a frequency. Cymatic frequencies affect texture, water, structure and much more. Cymatics is the study of visible sound and vibration. We, as humans, have an opportunity to directly affect our physical outcomes through our daily practices and expanding awareness. Frequency also can refer to how often something is repeated.

When we are in a state of low frequency, it might manifest as frustration, fear, anxiety, depression, headache, etc.

When we are in a state of high frequency, we feel happy, loved and fulfilled. Right now, you have the opportunity to learn how to elevate your own personal frequency. Raising your frequency and positive vibes is learning to recognize when we are NOT in a state of balance. This involves using focused breath-work, drinking more water, replenishing our magnesium and increasing our movement.

Entrepreneurs are those who have been pushing themselves for most of their lives and now are feeling the impact of the stresses in the body.

The trend moving into 2020 and beyond is that 50% of the workforce will be free-lancers, in one way or another.

How do I keep my edge and create balance, resulting in the greatest return on Investment?

Happiness and well-being equal HIGH FREQUENCY.

It is so important to routinely pull back from long hours, deadlines and high levels of stress. Take the opportunity to raise your frequency by investigating surfing, yoga, martial arts, hockey, playing a musical instrument, cooking, hiking, and the creative arts…. the list is endless.

Finally, create a healthy support network. Support comes from within yourself, your organization and outside your organization. Consider finding groups to associate with that are different genres - mix it up. Maybe look into mentoring, or even an internship program within your organization. You might be surprised at the overall exchange and outcome.

Frequency

$$Hz = O+H_2O+Mg+Movement:$$
Frequency = oxygen, water, magnesium & movement

Quantum physicist Nassim Haramein's findings are focused on "a fundamental geometry, space that connects us all; from the quantum and molecular scale to cosmological objects in the universe". (Resonance Science Foundation)

This space holds energy. Energy that you and I can control or manipulate through thought frequency. Energetic signatures and wave frequencies come from thought and emotion. These thoughts or beliefs (conscious or unconscious) are either helping us or hurting us. I call this the "Double H Principle". Consciously we can understand in a situation or experience this principle of Helping or Hurting, but unconsciously we may be sabotaging our desired outcome.

To raise our frequency, we want our 60 plus trillion cells to follow instructions! Let's just begin with a new awareness of our breath. I like the way Dina Proctor, author of Madly Chasing Peace, describes how she created disruption in her thoughts (conscious & unconscious) by stopping three times a day for 3 minutes to focus on Being still and breathing.

Is this meditation? Yes, one of many different types. Right now, let's take our smart phones, tablets, etc.. and program them with an alarm 3 times during the day.

Meditation and breathing exercises will help raise your frequency and positive vibes. At the same time, before you begin to breathe notice where your thoughts are or have been at the time – have they been in high vibration or low vibration?

Now take a moment and bring yourself into a higher vibration and notice the difference.

TAPPING
The Emotional Freedom Technique (EFT)

EFT is a commonsense approach reducing and eliminating unwanted behavior and patterns. There are no negative side effects. "EFT offers great healing benefits." –Deepak Chopra, MD

- No pulling or pushing the body
- No needles
- No surgical procedures
- No pills or chemicals

Because of the simplicity of this technique many are teaching it within their own constructs such as teachers with their students, coaches with their athletes, physicians with their patients and so on. The tapping results in neutralizing the unwanted feeling in a very short period of time.

Gary Craig, the founder of this technique www. Emofree.com, summarizes a session with a returning Soldier: "We taught the techniques to Rich so he could work on the rest of his war memories on his own time at home. Within a few days they were all neutralized. They no longer bothered him. As a result, the insomnia went away and so did the insomnia medication (under the supervision of his physician)."

This tapping technique will rock your world! EFT is based on the Chinese meridian systems in the body and has proven to have profound effects

Tapping Points

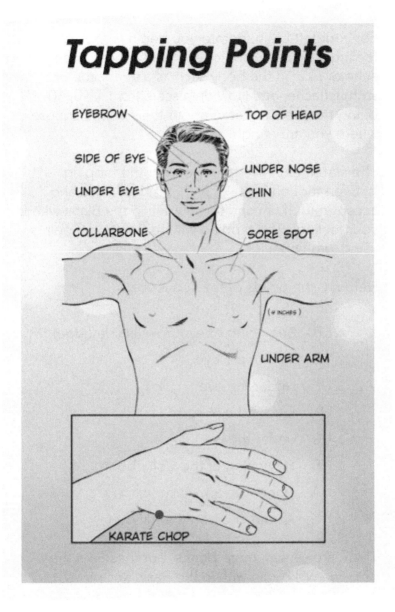

on the imbalances by balancing them. The more you practice this, the quicker the positive effect will arrive if and when you may need it in a crisis (example: panic attack). Let's keep this simple and give it a try. Repetition is the key.

For your left brain: Before you begin, choose a feeling such as frustration, anger, sadness or an ache or pain in the body such as a headache or stomachache, etc. Now on a scale from 1-10, 10 being the most agitated about this feeling, choose where you are at right now.

The statement I like to use during the tapping is: Even though I feel _____, I still love and accept myself unconditionally. Fill in the blank with your feeling. The tapping will be done on 8 points, using two fingers.

Here are the points of the sequence:

1. EB – Beginning of eyebrow (inside edge)
2. SE – Side of the eye
3. UE – Under the eye
4. UN – Under the nose
5. UL – Under the lip
6. CB – Beginning of the Collarbone
7. UA – Under the arm (armpit)
8. KC – Karate chop on the hand

There are several more points, but these are the ones we will begin with in the Basic Recipe.

As we begin to tap down one side of the body repeat the phrase during the tapping of each point, then go down the other side of the body. This equals ONE round. Check in with your number on the scale from 1-10. If it is not below a 2, do another round. We continue tapping down the left and right sides of the body until we are at a zero. Sometimes in the beginning, it may take up to 5 or 6 - rounds maybe more. Repetition is key.

According to Gary, 10-percent of the population suffers from one or more phobias. These phobias can create intense fear and severely limit the quality of life of those who have them. There are many possible phobias and EFT can be effective on all of them. Here is a list of a few:

Public speaking	The telephone
Heights	Marriage
Snakes, spiders & insects	Men
Claustrophobia	Failure
Dentists	Disease
Needles	Dogs
Driving	Computers
Elevators	Bees
Flying	Being alone
Bridges	Sex
Rejection	Water

Now consider the discovery statement on which EFT is built: The cause of all negative emotions is a disruption in the body's energy system.

Take-Away

Tapping is free

Repetition is key

Check Out: www.Emofree.com

Creating Life Balance

"Everything is energy and that's all there is to it. Match the frequency of your reality you want, and you cannot help but get that reality. It can be no other way. This is not philosophy. This is physics."

Albert Einstein

"Our questions can be powerful tools for learning, but only if they challenge our assumptions rather than confirm our beliefs."

Stephen Shapiro

Creating Life Balance

Oxygen
Are you breathing?

When we concentrate, oxygen usage is mainly in the brain. While increasing concentration we increase oxygen substantially. Stress does not support healthy concentration, because it is a diversion. Stress creates a need in the muscular system, increasing tension, which further increases oxygen demand. If our breathing is shallow, this will ultimately set us up for further imbalances in our body. The condition of our blood (made mostly of water) will determine the function and condition of the organs. When the blood is dirty, lacking oxygen, it has more carbon dioxide or waste. When our blood is filled with oxygen it is cleansed, thereby promoting optimal functioning from our heart, spleen, lungs, liver, muscles, and the skin.

First, stop for a moment and observe your breathing. Are you holding your breath, or taking short shallow breaths? Or are your breaths deep and even? Shallow, rapid breathing is a typical part of the stress response and can be especially distressing for people with anxiety. Stress is an extremely unhealthy condition, which causes the brain to release the chemical cortisol, and has been shown to reduce brain and organ function. Even unhealthy bacteria, germs, viruses and parasites love your body when there is oxygen deficiency! According to studies, your lungs will deteriorate 9-25% per decade unless you do something to maintain them.

The frequency and depths of our breathing have

a direct correlation to our state of well-being. We often override our feelings and our body's messages in order to get on with the task at hand. Each time you ignore your body & mind's promptings, you are building a higher wall & creating obstacles on the journey to reaching your full potential. Then, one day everything collapses! Take deep cleansing breaths throughout the day. Our body runs on oxygen!

When the body has ample oxygen, it produces enough energy to optimize your metabolism and eliminate accumulated toxic wastes in the tissues. Natural immunity is achieved when the immune system is not burdened with heavy toxic buildup.

Some of the symptoms of possible oxygen deficiency are:

- Overall body weakness
- Fatigue
- Circulatory problems
- Poor digestion
- Muscle aches and pains
- Dizziness
- Depression
- Irrational behavior
- Irritability
- Acidic stomach
- Lung problems
- Any chronic /long term disease
- Memory loss

Shallow breathing affects everything we do. By bringing awareness to our breath and practicing focused breath work we can improve our health and well-being.

Breathing is FREE and can be PRACTICED anywhere!

"Detoxification occurs when oxygen is introduced into the system."- Dr. Norman McVea

"Simply put, disease is due to a deficiency in the bodies oxidation process leading to an accumulation of toxins. These toxins would ordinarily be burned in normal metabolic functioning". -Dr. Albert Wahl.

The key to focused breath is not lying on the couch or sleeping. It is a mentally active process that leaves the body relaxed, calm and focused. Mastering your breathing will re-connect you to your body and mind, thereby stopping the stress response.

Where can you practice? Anywhere! At your desk, over lunch, while stopped at a traffic light, on the train, waiting for someone, climbing stairs or walking your pet.

A shortage of oxygen is a common factor in serious conditions such as asthma, emphysema, and bronchitis. The development of cancerous cells is one major consequence of severe oxygen starvation. Oxygen shortage in the human body has been linked to every major illness category including heart conditions, digestion and

elimination problems, respiratory disease, inflamed swollen and aching joints, sinus problems, yeast infections and even sexual dysfunction.
When our cells lack oxygen they weaken and die. Think about your latest stress situation. Did you feel any of those symptoms?

Controlled awareness to breathing can cause physiological changes that include lowered blood pressure and heart rate, reduced levels of stress hormones in the blood…reduced lactic acid build up in the muscle tissue when you work out, balanced levels of oxygen and carbon dioxide in the blood.

Are you breathing NOW? Of course, you are, but how are you breathing? Deep breathing increases the supply of oxygen to your brain – which promotes a state of calmness. This helps you feel connected to your body. It also brings awareness away from worries in your head and quiets your mind.

Deeper breathing can also help you with speaking, improve your immune system, increase your physical energy and increase feelings of calm and wellbeing. Slower, deeper breathing can keep you from overreacting in a situation and from doing something that can potentially hurt your relationships.

Let's breathe together… Place your hands on your ribcage, so you can feel your diaphragm expand

and contract. We will proceed to practice "Ocean Breath". This is done with your mouth open and is an audible breath. When done correctly, actually sounds like the ocean!

Breathe in and out....in and out.... Again, breathe in, hold it.... sip in a bit more air, and slowly exhale. Consider putting a post it note on your monitor, reminding you to remember to breathe.

Take-Away

Set your timer for 3 minutes.
If you go over 3 minutes great!
Let's just focus on 3 minutes 3 times a day

Find a space where you will not be distracted

Begin by saying to yourself
"breathe in - breathe out, count one."
Using this dialogue up to
the count of 10

Repeat 2 more times
(3 X 3 meditation)

It is normal for chatter to
come into your mind

Come back to the count

You are now practicing Focus!

Consider investing in an Oximeter -It measures
your oxygen saturation level in your body

I was preparing to travel to New York City to support Collete while she hosted a new television reality show when she introduced me to her director/producer Dani Davis over the phone. I found Dani to be one of the most creative people I have ever met, and I couldn't wait to be involved with her project. I invite you to read her story.

Dani's Story

It was winter. It was an unheated warehouse in Brooklyn, and we were shooting the first season of a television show I had created. The show, called Girl Starter, was a reality show. A competition show featuring 8 entrepreneurial young women, building businesses together, mentored by scions of business and finance, supported by several public companies' resources. Our intention was to inspire young women across America to exercise their own "starter" muscles and create community around assisting girls and young women in their efforts to make things happen. The young women selected for the show came from diverse backgrounds, and from across America. For many it was their first time in New York City, and for all, it was their first time on television. And it was a big production team - we numbered 130 people - again, all from diverse backgrounds, and on top of it, none of us had ever worked together. Charged with producing an exciting new 6-episode television series and shooting it in under 5 weeks, on a shoestring budget in a cold, not so clean warehouse in Greenpoint, we might have had a tough time. Stress on the young women featured on the show was high throughout our time in production, due to the demands not only of being on camera, but also to the demands of striving to build an exciting new business. But when we were all assembled on set in Greenpoint, magic happened. Every day!!

Our show's host, Collete Davis, a dynamic, charismatic, joyful, intelligent, fire ball of a person, brought her A Game with her, as well as her own secret to success, Susan Davis. I first met Susan in my kitchen just days before shooting started. It was suddenly cold in New York City, and Susan had arrived from Florida, where outerwear is at most a light rain jacket. I believe she walked into my house wearing a purple fake fur jacket that she had purchased just that afternoon at a flea market in Chelsea. She looked fabulous, very "downtown glam," and warm! Her eyes were bright with the promise of adventure in the big city.

We had dinner and conversation among the diverse group which was lively and all over the place! Susan was great at lobbing the phrase, "I can help you with that," and another, "Have you ever tried…" into the center of the chatter, which drove us deeper into exploration of our own production assistants - when energy or focus waned, Susan quietly and quickly to brought everyone back to the room and to each other. As a result, one could walk on set at Girl Starter and be greeted with smiles, hellos, and one would hear lots of laughter and joyful chatter in the breaks between takes. To be there was to feel energized and hopeful about all that was happening as well as what might come. There was a creativity that everyone felt a part of, and the presence of a true collaborative spirit among a group of people who had never been together in this setting before.

Susan introduced simple practices like "tapping" and breathing to Girl Starter. I might walk through a group of grips reloading radios and mics to see two of them tapping, re-energizing for the next session. The young women of Girl Starter had a series of exercises Susan created for them to which they could return at any time the stress became overwhelming and bring themselves swiftly to a place of focus and calm, so that they could do their best work. We called our Green Room the Magic Room. It was utterly nothing to look at - a cold, sort of dirty, curtained off area with a cheap pleather sofa, some office chairs, and a folding table. We had bottled water in there (actually, we had a lot of bottled water and seltzer from our sponsor - in fact so many palettes of the stuff occupied valuable space in our production office, that we used them as area dividers).

points of view, and ourselves. It was clear that Susan's energy could bring a kind of awareness and deepening of experience to any situation. I was intrigued enough to ask if she was planning to be with Collete on set, all in the hopes of determining if she might be available to play a larger role for the entire team. She told me that she was planning to be around as much as needed.

Little did she know...
That she would be with us on set every single day for nearly five weeks, hopping in to difficult, transitional moments for the young women, working with them individually, and as a group to clear obstacles like fear and confusion, to inspire their creative minds, and to build a basis of trust among them that made for a beautiful energy that carried them all through the long, exhausting days and weeks of production. The strain of being away from one's support system, thrust into a pressure cooker environment, on camera constantly, knowing that you are being watched, recorded, judged, and still having to imagine and build an entirely new business, in real time, again to be judged by audiences and iconic business leaders is intense on its easiest day. I honestly cannot imagine the young women taking this journey without Susan's stealthy support.

Susan worked with our production team - the producers, the camera operators, the grips, the

But I digress. Our guest stars - prominent business and media personalities - used the Green Room as their home base while on set with us. Their work was to mentor the young women in the building of their businesses, advise, offer constructive criticism, and ultimately determine, at the end of their time with us, which of the businesses being built by the girls should continue forward in competition. It was a big job, and one the guest stars took seriously. So seriously, in fact, that there were points of real stress as they faced having to make tough choices about the girls' fate. Susan was there. And these leaders of industry would tap and breathe with her, and talk, and open up to us and to each other about their hopes for the future of women in business, and about the power of the young women with whom they were engaged on Girl Starter. And magic happened!

Each guest star left not only the imprint of their beautiful work with the young women on camera but also left a gift of themselves, of continued tangible support for the young women, of subsequent opportunities for the young women beyond Girl Starter, of additional funding opportunities for the businesses the girls were creating. Not a single guest passed through that Green Room without leaving such an offering.

Magic!!

I attribute this magic to the power of the work

we did at Girl Starter to change the paradigm for women in business, and also to the open, collaborative space we created in production, to which Susan brought a foundational energy of essential joy.

Production of Girl Starter ended, and the show aired on Discovery and TLC. Audiences enjoyed the camaraderie they saw among the young women, the guest stars, and the buoyant discourse of the show's segments. It was a fun show to watch, as well as one that helped a lot of young women to imagine their own possibility as entrepreneurs.

I know for sure that we succeeded in reaching audiences because we had such a trusting environment on set, and I know that I am delighted that Susan was able to be with us. She worked with nearly 150 people in under five weeks, facilitating our process of creation. And she wasn't tired!

Speaking of tired, did you know that magnesium is essential to your well-being? Did you know that hydration is key to your feeling energized? Did you know that Epsom salt baths can heal a million ills? Susan does and she taught it to all of us.

As we moved away from production on Girl Starter, and into next phases, Susan's energy and commitment to the members of our team never waned. I was experiencing some feelings of anxiety and insecurity in my professional life, so she and I began to work together privately, as I explored blockages in my own past (both conscious and unconscious).

I found this work illuminating and enlightening. It was cleansing work for the brain and the soul, but was completely noninvasive, and entirely based on energy. Much like the work Susan did with the members of our Girl Starter team, this work provided a foundation for discovery of the best self, while energizing my spirit. One on one, Susan's voice and suggestions magically led me to places in my mind that were like small, dark, locked rooms. Once unlocked, the information held there was released, and I found a freedom of space in my brain, and in my emotions, that gave me room to create my next path in the world.

I found I was able to allow my own creativity to blossom. I found myself able to be courageous, to step into work about which I am truly passionate. In the year and a half since I last worked with Susan, I have returned to my work in the live theater, which I had left to build Girl Starter, and I find that I am energized, focused and that the work I am doing is very successful. There were many internal barriers keeping me from doing the work I most love to do. I find now that I see possibility far more than I see limitation.

Of particular use even now, as I have not worked with Susan in many months, is the 3 x 3 Meditation she teaches. This distills meditation down to a single word, focused on 3 times daily for 3 minutes each time. This is powerful and change making meditating and something I highly recommend, especially for those folks afraid of meditating for long periods of time. Focus on a single word inspires clarity, depth of understanding and subsequent simplicity, which can then lead to greater comprehension of complex issues. Magic.

I suppose it all comes down to healing, which with Susan around finds its way into most interactions, and gives people opportunity for energetic change in their work with each other, whether professional or personal - it is really all the same.

The other day I received a book that Susan had made for me, filled with beautiful photos she had taken during our production time on Girl Starter, brimming with inspirational quotes and thought starters. The love in this book leaps off the page - so many smiling faces, happy people, finding their way forward together! I loved seeing each face, experiencing each memory, knowing for sure that all pictured had a wonderful time making something wonderful. Perusing the pages of the book brought me to a healing space around my own experience of making that show and building that company. The power of Susan's heart, whether felt in person, over the telephone, or via the pages of a book, can be felt, and it heals the soul.

My wish for everyone is that they have the chance to experience the magic of the beautiful, ageless woman, whose bright light creates a field of joy around her and welcomes in those whose light could use a boost. I think it must be wonderful to be Susan, to see reflected in all those around her the healing power of her heart. I am grateful for her presence in my life.

Dani Davis
Director and writer
New York City

"Simply put, disease is due to the deficiency in the body's oxidation process leading to an accumulation of toxins. These toxins would ordinarily be burned in normal metabolic functioning."

Dr. Albert Wahl

Creating Life Balance

"All illness, physical, mental, emotional, physiological, are really the result of stress or imbalance of some type."

Norm Shealy, MD, PhD

Water

Do you know how much water you are drinking? Our bodies have a fundamental need for water. Water comprises of up to 60% of our bodies, exactly like Mother Earth! When our body is deprived of this natural resource, our toxic stress response kicks in. To calculate the formula for how much water we need, take your body weight and divide this number in half. This is the minimum ounces of water we should take in on a daily basis. So, if my weight were 200 pounds, then I would need a minimum of 100 ounces of water daily. Remember that other liquids such as energy drinks, caffeinated beverages and fruit juices do not count.

H2O helps our body temperature stay regulated. It also cushions our joints and acts as a transport for oxygen and nutrition by way of our cells. We are fortunate that water helps prevent blood pressure from dropping to critical levels. The more we have awareness to our water intake the more our bodies can benefit. Another added benefit is water definitely encourages elimination through bowel movement as well as helps the normal kidney function from getting impaired, lowering incidence of urinary tract infections (UTI).

Our skin is affected by how much water we consume. Adequate amounts of water keep us from premature aging and dry skin. Water also helps us from experiencing migraine or recurring headaches and helps alleviate fevers. To stimulate the immune system, use water in hydrotherapy, hot water and steam (such as in a sauna or whirlpool). The body has no way to store water and needs fresh supplies every day.

Nourish yourself! When you feel thirsty, you are already dehydrated. Yet most of us continue to push ourselves, ignoring the natural signals our body sends us to slow down and refuel. Begin today, with this new awareness of adding more water to your diet. Stop, take a breath, and listen to your body. Grab a nourishing snack and a big glass of water. Vow never again to skip a meal for the sake of "time." Replace sodas with water. Set reminders to take a break.

The following will absolutely amaze you:

- One glass of water shuts down midnight hunger pangs for almost 100% of the dieters participating in a University study.

- Lack of water is the #1 trigger for daytime fatigue.

- Preliminary research indicates that 8-10 glasses of water per day could significantly ease back and joint pain for up to 80% of those who suffer from this pain.

- A mere 2% drop in body water can trigger fuzzy short-term memory, trouble with basic math, and difficulty focusing on the computer screen.

- Drinking 5 glasses of water daily decreases the risk of colon cancer by 45%, plus it can slash the risk of breast cancer by 79%. One is also 50% less likely to develop bladder cancer.

- Are you drinking the amount of water you should every day?

Take-Away

Consider investigating new apps that remind you to drink water

Always carry a container for water with you, maybe one with a filter

Consider investing in a smart water bottle that will help remind you to drink

When you kindly remind others to increase their water intake you are reminding yourself

Up to 60% of the human adult body is water

According to H.H. Mitchell, Journal of Biological Chemistry 158 the brain & heart are composed of 73% water & the lungs are about 83% water

The skin contains 64% water, muscles & kidneys are 79% & even the bones are watery: 31%

"You can trace every sickness, every disease and every ailment to a mineral deficiency."

Linus Pauling
2-time Nobel Prize Winner

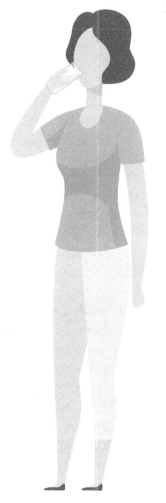

It was during the winter holiday season when I reconnected with Kim Hiser, a high school classmate, through social media. She had some concerns about her daughter, Lateesha, and the demands college life were giving her. I offered my help and Lateesha accepted, this is her story.

Lateesha's Story

I was first introduced to Susan through my mother while she was looking for a way to help me cope with all of my anxiety. I had pretty severe test anxiety yet felt fine with extreme situations such as emergency care. Things just didn't add up, I could remain calm with dangerous situations but hyperventilate and have panic attacks over papers. I refused to reach out for help because in my eyes everyone that I had surrounded myself with seemed like they had everything together. If they could get through it then all I had to do was suck it up and just get over it. If I needed any type of advice, I just asked within the family even though I knew they could only help me so far. While I love my family dearly, they were not the people who were going to be able to help me overcome long term problems with test anxiety, depression, paranoia of not being good enough, low self-esteem and much more. They thought everything was normal. What I didn't let them know was I had constant headaches because of terrible night terrors and endless amounts of stress being added due to all of the activities I had taken on.

I remember my mother talking to me over the phone after I just couldn't keep my emotions all bottled up anymore. She said that since she could not help me with my stress from so far away, she had found someone who would be able to. All I had to do was talk to this person (who I couldn't see and vice versa) over the phone. Mother told me a little bit about Susan's work and how it dealt with working on past life regression, I had no idea what that even meant. I would soon find out.

My first session with Susan was in the middle of my second semester at college, after I realized my mother was right and I really needed to get some help. All the anxiety from not doing as well as I would have liked was building up in a negative way. I picked a quiet spot in the dorms where I lived and called her. I was very guarded as to what I said to her at first because I was not even sure if this was going to help. How could talking about my fears make them go away? During my first session I felt totally safe. She couldn't see me so if I got emotional over some touchy topics, I would not feel embarrassed. After one hour of talking over the phone I felt such a great release, almost as if I had been carrying this huge emotional baggage that I just kept adding to. I felt lighter, happier and absolutely exhausted. After the session was done, I felt a warm blanket wrapped around me like I was not all alone anymore. It felt like that moment before you wake up from a wonderful dream where you are just humming with energy, or right after a really tough workout when your mind is calm, and your body is exhausted from all the work that it just put in.

We had worked through my headaches, night terrors, paranoia, worries and my anxiety about not being good enough–a lot of things in a short period of 60 minutes.

It almost felt too good to be true that so many of my problems I could just talk through. Talking to a stranger is hard especially when it is about sensitive subjects, but it felt like talking to an old friend, too natural to be awkward. I was never pushed to say anything, I only spoke about what I wanted to talk about and then worked through the things I told Susan. I learned more about myself from what I told her, than anyone had made me realize in my life. I was the one who could help myself when I started to feel super stressed; all I needed was the awareness to know when to stop myself.

Shortly after the first session I noticed a difference in my confidence, my attitude during lectures and how I took notes. My confidence in my athletic abilities had changed as well. I no longer felt weighed down during practice from not understanding lectures during the day. My mind was clear, and I could focus on what I loved most, being an athlete. It was a struggle some mornings. I had to constantly work on being positive and being mentally aware of the people that I was surrounding myself with. When I worked my thoughts were clearer. I knew what I wanted and now I had control over small things that turned poor grades into outstanding achievements. When I was studying for exams late into the night or early in the morning, I would do some tapping techniques given to me by Susan. If tapping was not enough to dispel all of the nerves before going to sleep, I listened to audio recordings of Susan talking about deep breathing and mental clarity. I had to believe in myself and when I gained that confidence, school, sleep and sports came easier.

Slowly I began to feel in control of my own life. I realized that I didn't have to measure my worth or brains against other people in my class. I learned differently and they learned another way. There were so many techniques Susan gave me to use but the most effective was mentally surrounding myself with my council of family and people I respected. I could ask them anything and they would help direct me towards the right path. If I needed to talk to someone about making a decision for school, I could call on this council and talk through what I was feeling. Life is stressful but growth is never achieved without some changes. It seemed that just as soon as I was getting my confidence back something would knock me back to where I began. While working on myself trying to figure out my place in the vast world I realized I had pushed aside important decisions. All the decisions that I had pushed aside came flooding up at once and it was overwhelming. I had never admitted to my family how bad my depression was. I just knew they would not understand.

As my life changed overnight my depression became uncontrollable and working with people began to give me anxiety. I never faced my depression or toxic relationships head on- I just talked about them. Now, with the tools that I had learned I would have to face them. A strong way to overcome my depression was to workout, being an athlete in college was extremely important to me to help keep my depression and anxiety at bay.

I had overcome a lot of obstacles in my earlier career by having two ACL surgeries that were not easy, but I had done it. Now trying to balance two degrees while doing two sports at the same time began to wear me down. My peers along with people I looked up to said I needed to lighten my load. I knew if I stopped being an athlete that the rest of my mental sanity would go out the window. I couldn't drop my degrees either because they were going to launch me into my actual career in life. When I found myself without the ability to keep moving forward and felt stuck, I would call Susan who would help me gain clarity. She would remind me that breathing, and water intake were key, all I had to do was stop, breath and everything would begin to clear.

Before exams or athletic meets I would refocus my thoughts and positive energy on techniques taught by Susan, visualizing down to the most minute detail what my day would be like. I would visualize the races and the outcome I wanted. I would run over these many times in my head, never doubting for a moment that what I visualized would come true. After having success with visualizing for athletic events I turned it around and used visualization in the classroom. I went over the exams in my head from start to finish, envisioning walking into the exam room, getting the exam and knowing how long it would take. I imagined getting stuck on a question and asking my personal council for help. I made sure through the exam that I practiced taking water breaks, and finally I envisioned walking out of the exam room feeling confident. Knowing what kind of grade, I would get on the exams. This motivated me to study certain material from lectures that I believed would be on the exams. The success was profound. There is not a better feeling than to hear your professor ask what you are doing different; my grades were night and day different.

Now that school and sports were going well, I needed to work on getting better with my relationships in life. One relationship had become so toxic; I didn't realize I had begun to compromise my important core values. I was so blind that I felt that I had to keep this person in my life, that in order to feel alive, I had to deal with the stress that this relationship brought on because somehow, I deserved it. I could not do any better. This fear held me back and made me believe that I wouldn't find anyone. I was lowering my self-esteem and my worth.

The people around me didn't know because I hid the truth. But inside I knew that this relationship was not ok. The few people that did know I ignored. I thought that if I just tried harder, I could make it work. It was almost a challenge to prove them wrong. I would make the relationship work even if it sacrificed my own happiness and values along the way. After trying so hard to make my relationship work, I came to the conclusion that I couldn't keep up the fake facade anymore, I felt hollow when I looked in the mirror. I was so tired of trying to please everyone and in one moment of self-confidence, my whole vision of myself changed.

I had been so focused on making people around me think everything was ok that I didn't recognize myself anymore. I hated myself even more when I knew I should have stuck to my beliefs, but instead I crumbled. If I couldn't look at myself and feel ok at my reflection how could I show that to other people? This relationship had messed with my self-image so much that I closed myself off to people and never allowed my outer appearance to look weak. I changed the subject when people asked how I was, I just pretended everything was perfect. After a few months I couldn't hide it from myself- I couldn't pretend any longer. I had to face that my depression was once again dragging me down and that I needed to reach out for help again or all my effort of getting better would be for nothing.

The word depression has such a vast meaning and yet is often misunderstood. It can mean so many different things and it changes with each person. No one is the same so it's only fair to say that depression looks different on each person. To some depression can be sadness- it could mean a moment of feeling lost. And for others it could mean floating in a black sea alone, afraid to even move. Only in private moments would I even think about the demon I was battling. I thought it was selfish to ask for help especially since everyone is facing their own demons. My demon eventually began to win all of the time and I knew that if I didn't reach out for help that I would give up and lose. When I reached out to Susan again it was the most vulnerable, I had ever felt in front of someone, even if it was over the phone. I had never felt more beat down and I knew I was the one who had brought myself to this level. I had such a negative opinion of myself that I no longer cared about important things, such as being a better student and striving for excellence. I just didn't care, period.

It was a grounding moment when I told someone how I was feeling. I didn't want to be told that I was crazy for having these feelings, but it was the only answer I thought they would give me. Or maybe they would tell me I was broken and not worth fixing. Maybe I would have to take a bunch of medication in order to feel better. I had already thought up a bunch of scenarios. What I wasn't prepared for was the process of working through my feelings and that I could feel better in doing that. I didn't have to take drugs to feel better and I wasn't going to be locked up somewhere just because of how I felt, I began to see that maybe my body was just unbalanced and that's why I couldn't get over this feeling of drowning.
I had so many unhealthy feelings that I didn't have to carry with me because they didn't belong to me. I saw how over time I had put standards for myself that were brought on by other people. I finally realized after working with Susan that I didn't have to live up to what other people expected of me. What really mattered was moving forward and working on things I wanted that mattered to me. Even though it sounds simple, it was so hard. I had always done what other people thought I should, but I was never really happy, never fully satisfied. I spent so much time being worried about offending other people

and constantly walking on eggshells that I forgot about myself. I tried to be other people and not myself. There is nothing wrong with learning from someone better, but it becomes a problem when you lose yourself along the way–like I did.

Acknowledging my depression and talking through it helped me grow. It alleviated my anxiety, helped me overcome bad relationships and made me a wiser woman. I never would have gotten to where I am today if I hadn't talked to Susan. Through her I learned to let go of past experiences, tackled hard life problems in the present and to embrace the wonderful future I was running toward. As a young adult there are plenty of challenges to overcome with everyday stress, but I was able to be a two-sport athlete with a double major while feeling like I was on the right path. I know now that in order to feel alive all I have to do is breathe and keep looking forward.

Lateesha Hiser is a recent graduate from Ripon College WI. While in college she was a two-sport athlete competing in Swimming, as well as Track & Field. She was conference champion for swimming in the 50 Free as well as Hammer Champion for Track and Field in her respective NCAA Division.

She earned two bachelor's degrees in religion and Biology. When she isn't working out or studying, she loves to go hiking in the mountains, fishing, big game hunting and enjoys reading adventurous books.

"(I) Came back to mindfulness to sustain high performance—my own and my employees'."

Evan Williams
Twitter Co-Founder

"We do not stop playing because we grow old, we grow old because we stop playing."

Benjamin Franklin

Magnesium

What does a magnesium deficiency look like?

According to Dr. Norm Shealy, MD, PhD, Neurosurgeon with over 30 years of peer-reviewed research, magnesium deficiency is associated with all known disease.

Stress affects magnesium levels and show up as:

- Muscle cramps, twitches and tremors.

- Mental disorders including apathy, depression and anxiety.

- Osteoporosis

- Fatigue and muscle weakness

- High blood pressure

- Asthma

- Irregular heartbeat

When we are worried or stressed, we are in the process of depleting our magnesium stores. How does this feel? It may feel like anxiety, irritability and sleeplessness. This can create a loop effect, where we worry or look for outside reasons for this feeling. This depletes our magnesium further.

Many of the substances we consume daily deplete

our body's supply of magnesium, such as white sugar, flour, and caffeine. Also, unseen chemicals, such as fluoride and chlorine in our water have a negative effect on our magnesium levels.

Are you one of the lucky people who live near the ocean where a lot of magnesium is naturally in the air? Do you eat foods rich in magnesium, such as leafy greens, avocados, nuts, and best of all, dark chocolate? Is your life blissfully stress-free? Do you consume minimal amounts of sugar or caffeine? If you answered yes to any or all of these questions, then you are already ahead of the game.

One of the most easily recognizable symptoms of magnesium deficiency is muscle cramps. Did you know half of all heart attack patients receive injections of magnesium chloride to help stop the blood clotting and calcification of the arteries? Magnesium was considered the original "chill pill" back in the day with the average American intake in 1905 of 400 mg daily, and only 1 % of Americans had depression prior to age 75.

While many people who suffer from hypertension already understand the need for balance of sodium and potassium, we could be missing the magnesium link! Magnesium is essential for calcium and potassium assimilation. If the calcium level within the cell is too high the muscles in the arterial walls will contract. Magnesium causes these muscles to dilate.

When calcium levels are high and magnesium levels are low this can cause us to become obese, with significant weight gain around the stomach. This could be a recipe for high blood pressure, diabetes and secretion of insulin, all known factors contributing to heart attack.

The evidence is accumulating to support that the lack of vitamin D may also contribute to magnesium deficiency. As we apply the UV sun block (filled with other hazardous chemicals) we are affecting our assimilation of Vitamin D. We should consider getting 20 minutes of sunshine in the morning or early evening before the heat is unbearable. If this is not possible, at least consider taking a D3 supplement.

Another source contributing to magnesium deficiency is the use of diuretics, which cause the wasting of potassium, which leads to the loss of magnesium. All of this information is becoming better understood. Many small clinics and private practitioners have taken on the ability to test for a full range of deficiencies, using a hair analysis or saliva test.

A lack of magnesium tends to magnify the stress reaction, making the problem worse. Some other causes of magnesium deficiency include diet, alcohol consumption, chronic stress, poorly controlled diabetes, excessive or chronic vomiting and/or diarrhea.

Let's create a new awareness for those food sources that contain magnesium, such as spinach, soybeans, pumpkin seeds and oat bran, as well as utilizing magnesium lotion or soaking in Epsom salts.

Some safety factors to keep in mind about magnesium supplementation: you should have normal kidney function; you do not have bowel obstruction, bradycardia, and myasthenia gravis or if you have kidney disease check with your doctor. Besides soaking in Epsom salts or using a topical magnesium lotion, you may consider adding nuts, green vegetables, black-eyed peas and spinach into your diet.

Resource - The Magnesium Miracle by Dr. Carolyn Dean MD

*In addition, eating too much calcium interferes with the absorption of magnesium, setting the stage for magnesium deficiency.

Take-Away

Epsom Salt Baths

Magnesium Lotion

Magnesium Supplements

**20 minutes of sun or
daily vitamin D3**

"Ten years of studies analyzing how our genes are affected by different practices such as mindfulness, yoga, meditation, and Tai Chi and found that they: don't simply relax us; they can 'reverse' the molecular reactions in our DNA which cause ill-health and depression"

The Journal. Frontiers in Immunology

"You never know how the next person you meet might be able to open doors for you. So always be kind, be generous, and be willing to go the extra mile."

Tiffany Pham

Movement with Intention

When I think about movement, so many enjoyable activities come to mind, like walking, running, biking, skiing, ice skating, swimming, etc.

How much movement do you have in your daily routine?

Maybe you have heard that, health-wise sitting is the new smoking!

So, let's begin to think about how and when we are going to start moving.

I love the idea of the stand-up desk to keep your core engaged while working. Ergonomic chairs are also worth investigating. But what I really want you to do is to take a good, hard look at how, and how often, you move.

You may be thinking, "I don't have time for exercise." We should all make movement a priority daily.

What happens when you move?

ONE
Your muscles use glucose to contract and utilize adenosine triphosphate, or ATP. Our bodies have small amounts of glucose & ATP stored, but when we move, we use up these stored supplies and create the need for more oxygen to make more ATP. Additional blood is then pumped into the muscles, providing them with extra oxygen. When

we are not taking in enough oxygen, lactic acid
will then accumulate. Normally, this lactic acid will
be removed from the body, approximately an hour
after the workout. As the muscles tear down, this
helps them to become stronger. The soreness felt
after the movement allows us to know our muscles
are gaining strength and flexibility.

TWO
Your oxygen intake will continue to build as you
increase the movement. You may need up to 15
times more oxygen during your workout, as you
begin to inhale and exhale more quickly. The
extreme limit of oxygen intake and utilization is
called "Vo2 max". We all need a higher Vo2 max.

THREE
When you add movement to your list of daily
priorities, the heart rate expands and moves the
blood at a faster pace filling it with oxygen. This
contributes to a lower resting heart rate (less
anxiety). In addition, this strengthens developing
blood vessels.

FOUR
Our brains benefit from this immensely. With more
blood flow, our brains will help us feel more alert
and grounded. This consistent movement supports
the brain and helps to reduce or eliminate
any potential mind threatening diseases. This
activity helps with the discharge of dopamine,
glutamate, GABA and serotonin. Serotonin is a
neurotransmitter, contributing to balance or state
of calm and well being.

FIVE

Your memory will improve, and as your body warms up it will release toxins through sweating.

SIX

Strength and flexibility within your body will show up as empowerment in your life, career, relationships, etc. Movement gives us the 'edge' and connection between body and brain. This means we will have clear mental capacity, making decision-making easier and removing brain fog.

Just begin to have the awareness as to how important movement is to your quality of life.

Ask yourself
'What kind of movement will I do today?'

There are so many applications today to help us remember to move.

I invite you to look at Notch, Fitbit, Jawbone's UP, Nike's Furlband, LUMOback and of course Smartwatches. And say to yourself "I AM open to moving my body in different ways."

There is so much more about movement to share! Check out Adam Sinicki, TheBioneer.com – simply amazing!

Take-Away

Start a new work-out class

Go on that hike

Try out a fitness app

Consider practicing yoga or martial arts

"If necessity is the mother of invention, exponential change is the mother of reinvention."

Nick Davis
VP, Corporate Innovation at
Singularity University

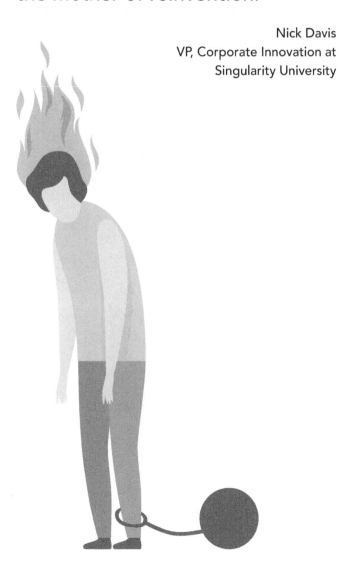

"If good people are asked to work in a bad culture, one in which leaders do not relinquish control, then the odds of something bad happening go up."

Simon Sinek

Relationships

The quality of your relationships determines your personal and professional success, the clients you attract for your business, your financial security, your happiness, your health and your overall well-being. Your relationships are the foundation for what you construct in every area of your life.

Support comes from within yourself, your organization and outside your organization. Building a healthy support network is a crucial–and fun–part of this process. Consider finding groups to associate with that are comprised of different genres – mix it up. Maybe look into mentoring, or even a volunteer program within your organization or community. You might be surprised at the overall exchange and outcome. These diverse networks can greatly affect you personally and professionally in the following areas:

For example, volunteering provides many benefits, both physically and mentally. The social contact aspect of helping and working with others can have a lifelong and profound effect on your overall psychological well-being. A meaningful connection to another person, working with pets or other animals, has also been shown to improve mood and reduce anxiety and stress.

Volunteering keeps you in regular contact with others and helps you develop a solid support system, which in turn protects you from developing depression.

By measuring hormones and brain activity, researchers have discovered that being helpful to others delivers immense pleasure. Human beings are hard-wired to give to others. The more we give, the happier we feel. Try it! You are doing good things for others and the community, which provides a natural sense of accomplishment. Your role as a volunteer can also give you a sense of pride and identity. And the better you feel about yourself, the more likely you are to have a positive view of your life and future goals. This is one of those 'raise your frequency' experiences.

Whatever your age or life situation, volunteering can help take your mind off your own worries, keep you mentally stimulated, and add more excitement to your life. Volunteering can also lessen symptoms of chronic pain and reduce the risk of heart disease.

The benefits of mentoring are many, and they may differ from program to program. Upper management and prospective mentors and those being mentored take notice of the possibility of mentorship. While mentoring, it allows the mentor to give back to the person being mentored as well as to the organization. It is great exercise in active listening, a leadership skill, and encourages the sharing of knowledge, this, in turn, gives you a sense of self–worth.

Mentoring also helps increase emotional intelligence and interpersonal skills and orients an individual to other areas within an organization or community. Maybe you are the person being mentored. What better way to learn than actively working to increase your knowledge and your network? Increased confidence and interpersonal skills are a plus, while also picking up any unspoken rules. Mentoring is the perfect way to convey your investment in others and bring more positive outcomes into your environment.

Your ability to build healthy new relationships (which bring you the outcomes you desire) is a direct result of what has occurred in your past relationships. These past experiences are stored in your subconscious mind, and also within your bodily cells. Many of these experiences are part of outdated paradigms, which are not relevant for your life as it is right now. They are like obsolete computer programs that are constantly running in the background, freezing up, slowing down your conscious efforts. Because the truth is your subconscious mind is very much like a computer. It needs constant updating, so that it can create the results you desire. As you release old, toxic programs you prevent them from sabotaging your future.

And that's exactly what we do with the Resolution Experience. We lay the groundwork, so you can build the relationships and life-situations that bring you the success you deserve, both professionally and personally. We learn to work within our more challenging existing relationships, to refine them and make them work for us, instead of against. When we deal with opposing personalities, we are given an opportunity to practice mindfulness. Every moment is an opportunity.

Wouldn't you like to be blissfully abundant in all areas of your life?

Take-Away

**Consider checking out different
'Meet-up' groups to join**

**Mentorship - mentoring others
& finding a mentor**

Volunteer

Release toxic relationships

"Now that mindfulness meditation has become scientific, it has been demystified. It's going to be seen as fitness for the mind."

Chade-Meng Tan
Google Engineer & Search
Inside Yourself Pioneer

"Our thoughts are mainly controlled by our subconscious, which is largely formed before the age of 6, and you cannot change the subconscious mind by just thinking about it. That's why the power of positive thinking will not work for most people. The subconscious mind is like a tape player. Until you change the tape, it will not change."

Bruce Lipton

I met Charlene and David Litteral through professional and social forums at Fort Carson, Colorado during my husband's assignment there. I found them both to be exemplary leaders within our military community. I am thankful for their service.

David's Story

I spent my entire adult life in military service. That's not where my story begins and it's not where my story ends. But it is the period of my life that defined me. My dad was a divorcee who had been married twice before my mom. As such, I had siblings from his first two wives.

The two oldest siblings were out on their own when I came into my consciousness. I am referring to the time when you can start remembering your first memories. The third sibling was six years older than I and she lived with us. My dad would have four boys with my mom. So, the nucleus of our home consisted of two parents and five kids living in the home. I was the proverbial middle child.

My dad served during both the Second World War and the Korean War. From one little area, my dad, his brother, their uncle, and five cousins were all drafted at the same time. Fortunately, they all returned from the war.

It was a lifelong regret for my dad that he only possessed an 8th grade education. Many of the young men who came home from war took advantage of the GI Bill. Dad already had a family and kids; going back to school was not an option for him. His parents were very proud but penniless sharecroppers. It is likely most of the students at school in the mid-1930's came from families with money. Decades later when I asked my dad if I should take the ACT, Dad replied, "College is for rich kids, and you aren't rich." He worked for Ford Motor Company in a factory for 30 years and provided well for his family.

My Mom met Dad just before graduating high school and they eloped later that summer. Despite his lack of formal education, my Dad was one of the smartest, most genuine men, a person could ever hope to call friend. That said, Dad wasn't the greatest at helping his kids figure out what they wanted to be when they grew up.

When Dad told me that college was for rich kids, I joined the military with plans to use the tuition benefits to achieve my career goals. I ended up enlisting as a Combat Medic despite my aversion to blood. I would meet a girl with whom I would fall in love and get married before I left for Basic Training. We married on the afternoon on the night I graduated from high school.

The Army sent me to a variety of locations.

Probably the most important was my assignment as a Flight Medic in 1982. Most of our missions were what we called "ash and trash." Point of Injury missions were all but unheard of.

And then I had one. We were called to the scene of US Special Forces soldiers who had parachuted into the Black Forest. Their landings were marred by a lieutenant with near fatal chest injury and a senior sergeant with a compound fracture of the lower leg. I was so scared on the flight to the accident scene that I was trembling. My crew chief leaned over and reassured me, "You got this." I learned a lot about trusting others that night as those men put their lives into my hands as I had put my trust in my crew chief. A few months later, I flew to the scene of my first fatality. The first thing that struck me when I arrived on scene was the finality of that young man's life. He was undeniably dead, and I had other patients who were critically injured who needed my help. Still, I couldn't help but think of the soldier who was the same age as I and had the same number of children. It was a sobering realization of my own mortality. There would be more fatalities in peacetime and war.

A million miles and twenty-five years later, I found myself as the Command Sergeant Major of the storied 10th Combat Support Hospital about to deploy to Iraq. One might equate a Combat Support Hospital (referred to as CSH- pronounced "cash") to the Korean War Mobile Army Surgical

Hospital, the 4077th MASH, television series. Notwithstanding the improvements of modern medicine, there were some similar characters, although, if you came to my CSH looking for Hawkeye Pierce and Major Hulahan, you would be very disappointed. My CSH was a disciplined CSH.

On one assignment the Army sent me to Fort Campbell, Kentucky to the be the Command Sergeant Major of a large Army hospital taking care of the great warriors of the 101st Airborne Division (Air Assault) and their families. I have to admit, I was beginning to grow tired physically, and emotionally. I was 45-years old and had put a lot of miles on my body running physical fitness training. As I slid into the daily routine of staff meetings, training meetings, and ceremonies, it was easy to lose sight of the issues occurring at the soldier level. I have always thought that soldiers were important, hell, I was one too. My outlook changed one morning as we were conducting a change of command ceremony at the hospital. One of our soldiers failed to report for work that morning. When his sergeant went to the soldier's room to investigate, he found the soldier had placed a pistol against his own chest and pulled the trigger. It was not the first suicide I had seen. It was however, the first one of my soldiers who had taken his own life. Standing with my chaplain as we watched the grieving mother and father weep over the body of their son, I couldn't help but reflect on what I didn't know about that young soldier. There would be others.

A few months later our hospital lost a nurse-anesthetist to suicide in the workplace. He came to work in same-day surgery, went into the bathroom, started an IV on himself, and injected himself with a lethal dose of a paralytic agent. Shortly after that one of our soldiers drank himself to death and died in his girlfriend's apartment. As one can imagine, the mixture of anger and frustration was nearly unbearable. Two weeks later one of our wounded warriors got into some trouble and spent a night in jail. Before we could assess what was going on, his mother sprang for bail, and his girlfriend and buddy picked him up at the jail. While his girlfriend was outside smoking a cigarette, the soldier went into the bathroom, placed his belt around his neck and hung himself. Four days after his memorial service, another one of our wounded warriors died of an overdose of pain medication at home in a recliner. My commander and I declared an immediate stand-down. We enlisted all of the chaplains and mental health professionals we could find and conducted a day of mental health promotions- because that seemed like the thing to do. The following week, I left for the 10th CSH.

As I mentioned before, I arrived at the historic 10th Combat Support Hospital with full knowledge that we would be going to Iraq within a year. Our training was tough. We knew in Iraq we would be going to a group of fixed concrete facilities. Even so, we had to train with our mobile systems just in case another contingency occurred prior to our deployment. A few years earlier, one of our sister units was weeks away from deploying to Iraq when it was directed to deploy to Louisiana in support of the recovery after Hurricane Katrina. After closing up shop in Louisiana, they returned to their home base and deployed to Iraq. It was a true testament to the individual soldier.

At Fort Carson, we were getting to know all of our soldiers. Some of them were closer to us than others. In other words, we saw some on a daily basis, others only once a week. We had a few bad apples that needed to be out of the Army, and we put them there. Others had problems that we felt we could handle. One such case was a 30-plus year-old soldier who threatened to kill his chain of command. We had him placed on a mental health hold. Upon his release he seemed to be doing fairly well until he got cocky and started taunting his chain of command. I brought him into my office and within minutes, he began to talk of suicide. Once again, we had him hospitalized. Upon his release he bought a gun and early one morning, posted an email to me, the commander, a chaplain, and a couple of elected officials, decrying his maltreatment, and finally stating that he had just killed himself. I sent the staff duty officer and the military police to his room and when they knocked on his door, he placed a gun under his chin and pulled the trigger. The soldier lived for a few hours before succumbing to his wounds. Some of his fellow soldiers felt that the commander and I were responsible as did the post-commanding general. An investigation was initiated which is standard practice for any untimely death of a service member.

My head was spinning. Our command team was just getting into a good battle rhythm and we were only 60 days from deploying. Two weeks earlier, my dad died, and I spent a week with my mom and brothers grieving the loss of the greatest man in my life. My commander came into my office within a day or two of the suicide. He said he had someone he wanted me to meet. Her name was Susan Davis. Her husband was the commanding general's chief of staff and she had heard what we were going through. She wanted to help us. Moreover, she wanted to help me.

I have met some phenomenal people throughout my travels in the Army. But crossing paths with Susan was both surprising and refreshing. She was empathetic to what we were going through and immediately came up with suggestions for helping our entire organization. In addition to signing on to be my life-coach (I have had numerous role models and mentors but never a life-coach), Susan wanted to give each of our soldiers the experience of being personally responsible for their well-being. It is probably hard to visualize a giant room with over a hundred soldiers lying around on the floor breathing to the commands of Susan Davis- but it happened. It was a surreal scene that was repeated several times over the weeks preceding our eventual departure. She wanted to help each of us tap into our own reserve of resilience. It might seem counterintuitive that soldiers would need this type of intervention. However, most people don't understand the nature of the Iraq War and that being a soldier assigned to a fixed hospital in the middle of the International Zone (or one of our four other locations) means, you stay. While you are getting attacked with rockets or mortars, you stay. In an infantry unit, you shoot, move, and communicate. In a Combat Support Hospital, you can't shoot back at those who sent the mortars because they are too far away. You can't move because you can't leave your patients. All you can do is communicate... and stay. It takes a lot of guts and it wears on one's nerves.

After Susan's interventions we held a team-building event wherein we asked the soldiers to come up with the precepts of our charter. It was an agreement, of sorts, that we would sign onto to get us through our year in the Combat Zone. During our deployment we had a few soldiers exhibit bad behavior. Most were corrected with minor adjustments. A few were sent home. Overall, most soldiers thrived during our deployment.

I feel confident in stating that Susan Davis helped give our soldiers the key to unlock their inner strength, although most of them probably never realized it. We returned from our journey to Iraq the day after Thanksgiving 2009. Many of us are still friends today. Many of us forged a bond that will forever link us together.

It was my intention to retire upon bringing my soldiers home. The Army had different plans. I received a phone call from the Command Sergeant Major of the US Army Medical Command. She said, "Dave, we want you to be the Commandant of our Army Medical Department Noncommissioned Officers' Academy." I consulted my wife and we agreed to accept the challenge of going back to Fort Sam Houston and leading the premier enlisted medical leadership academy. Little did I know, I would be calling on Susan Davis one more time.

The first year at the academy was challenging, as we were modernizing our programs and developing new models for the Army, I was also preparing for the biggest single change of my life, my retirement. So, I was feeling worn down and nearly out of gas. One cold morning while I was cleaning up after physical fitness training, I received a phone call from the local Army Medical Center. They had one of my soldiers in the Emergency Room in cardiac arrest. Unfortunately, she did not make it. She was 7-years my junior and had experienced cardiac arrest while running individual PT with a couple friends.

Many people have seen movies depicting the knock on the door delivering bad news. I have had that solemn honor of performing that task. What most people have never seen are the challenges to leadership to find out where the soldier lived, the name of their next of kin, and lastly, sitting down to write the letter to the next of kin. In an ordinary unit in the Army those letters are written by commanding officers. In an academy, it is the sole responsibility of the Commandant. Feeling somewhat overwhelmed with myriad of tasks surrounding the passing of one of my staff members, I reached out to my life coach. Once again, she was there to talk, listen, advise, and counsel. She re-lit the personal spark that was dimming as I neared my retirement. Though she never called it The Quintessential Level, Susan understood what Plato referred to as the thumos or the spiritedness within man.

There are many levels in our modern society. Leaders must develop a keen understanding of the thumos or that quintessential level in each person. It is there where passion meets behavior. It is not only essential for leaders to understand it in the people they lead but also within themselves. Susan's methodologies were effective for my troopers and me. Many of them are still serving around the globe. Some are retired now and are spending time pursuing their lives' passions. A few are no longer with us but are missed.

David J. Litteral is a Command Sergeant Major, United States Army (Retired) MA.

"One of the most powerful ways to improve your health and enhance your performance is to get a good night's sleep."

Chris Johnson & Matt Johns

"Sleep deprivation and disrupted sleep schedules have been linked to increased risk for several cancers, most notably colon and breast cancer."

Kevin Loria/Business Insider

Sleep Deprived

What is the opposite of movement with intention? The answer is NO movement with intention or quantified sleep. Yes, lack of sleep contributes to stress, creating havoc with circadian rhythms, immune health and metabolism. We have a 24-hour daily internal clock that is always running between sleepiness and alertness.

This is Circadian Rhythm. For most of our biggest dip in our energy occurs in the middle of the night between 2:00–4:00am or just after lunch at 1:00-3:00pm. Our circadian rhythm needs regular sleep habits. Consider going to bed at the same time and waking at the same time.

Sometimes a sporting event, or time change, or even jet lag can disrupt our circadian rhythm. This contributes to making it more difficult to focus and maintain being at the top of your game.

We should be spending about one-third of our time sleeping. Sleep is just as important as food and water!

Without enough sleep it is difficult to maintain and form pathways in our brain to continue to learn, as well as creating difficulty in our response time and concentration.

There is no magic number of sleep hours; in general, more people are getting less sleep than needed due to longer work hours and social media distraction.

A few outcomes of being sleep deprived are:

- High blood pressure

- DNA disruption

- Risk of diabetes

- Cardiovascular health

- Increased obesity

- Aging skin

- Risk of stroke

The University of Chicago Medical Center discovered that after 3 nights of not sleeping contributed to irregular blood sugar levels. And according to the European Heart Journal losing sleep can increase your chances of cardiovascular disease by 48 percent!

Chronic sleep loss can create dysfunction in glucose metabolism and appetite regulation setting up individuals for unwanted weight gain. There is also a direct link to quality of sleep, skin function and aging.

The most profound statistic that could keep you up at night is the fact that busy adults who get less than 6 hours of sleep have an increased chance of stroke by 4 times. Re: University of Alabama

So how can we increase our quality of sleep?

Take-Away

Set a schedule to go to bed &
wake up at the same time

Consider adding an application to your
devices to change the blue screen to
yellow

Time to get moving...Exercise

Practice mindfulness, & learn to meditate

Track your sleep through smart technology

Avoid caffeine & nicotine & heavy or
spicy meals before bedtime

Investigate melatonin supplements

Create a dark, quiet, cool space to sleep

"Through our emotional states and the automatic behaviors they produce, we continue to create the present to be like the past through an unconscious state that doesn't require thought or use of choice and free will."

Linda Gadbois

"You can do anything as long as you have the passion, the drive, the focus and the support."

Sabrina Bryan

The Resolution Experience

Past Life Resolution – The Resolution Experience
Susan Davis, ThM

We have seen an increasing interest in holistic healing methods in the West for several reasons. Some of this interest is due to the fact that people are dissatisfied with traditional methods of medicine. Traditional Medicine may be different for audiences, depending on where they live. It's not clear what it is as it may be traditional now for us but not for Chinese people, etc. Most people call it western medicine, I believe, although that's also strange. The Resolution Experience uses the process of educating and motivating people to take responsibility for their health and personal relationships.

As a person begins to explore patterns of behavior within themselves or other family members, it becomes obvious that there are roles being played such as protector, leader, helper, victim, teacher, lover, parent and obedient child – just to name a few. Along with these roles, feelings of helplessness, nervousness, anger, uncertainty, insecurity, vulnerability, alienation, betrayal and anxiousness may prevail. In conjunction with the roles and feelings, symptoms such as stomachaches, headaches, high blood pressure, throat constriction, vision problems, confusion, muscle tension, breathing problems and the desire to run or escape may manifest.

Past Life Therapy/Resolution differs from other

forms of regression techniques in that it is not generally used just for past life exploration and knowledge seekers. Past Life Resolution is performed with specific therapeutic target(s) as the result. This method does not require formal induction or hypnosis. In fact, it typically uses so-called "de-hypnosis" techniques or "focused–state" to access unresolved past experiences. This modality helps resolve past life survival scripts (patterns), that may be affecting one's state of mind, behaviors, and mental and physical health in this (or even future) lifetime. Among the pioneers in this field are Morris Netherton and Karl Schlotterbeck.

Many people do not understand the true meaning of the term "Past Life." It does not require a belief in reincarnation or requires us to regress to previous lifetimes. Any time prior to the current day is actually considered "Past Life" … 5 days ago, 5 years ago, 50 years ago or 500 years ago! Dr. Netherton has been using and teaching these techniques for over 40 years, and they have been proven to have powerful results in a significantly reduced time period, compared to traditional counseling techniques. An aside to this discussion is the fact that this modality is consistently helping adults and children of all ages.

Coping with problems is not solving problems. It is another way of saying, "I'm adapting to this problem that I can't totally resolve."

Some significant areas where the Resolution Experience is traditionally used are:

- Troubled behavior and attitude patterns that have persisted over time, despite repeated attempts to change.

- Relationships dynamics that seem to have a life of their own (intense attraction/aversion to another person, deep seated issues that defy resolution).

- Phobias – intense fears, such as fear of heights or fear of water, that seem unconnected to an experience in the current life.

- Some chronic physical ailments, sensations and pain.

- Dominate attitudes or emotions that seem to persist throughout your life.

The Resolution Experience can positively affect practically all areas of our life.

My intent is to share this technique, "The Resolution Experience," with as many people as possible. I know this is one of the best modalities to enhance the wellness of individuals as well as our communities.

After all, we are all connected; and what benefits an individual will potentially benefit the collective whole.

In-house Mindfulness Coaching & Professional Development

Consistent coaching offers a significant return on investment (ROI) for companies. The ICF Global Coaching Client Study found the 86 percent of companies made back at least their investment.

Consistent Coaching Can:

• Assist organizations with key business goals.

• Bolster creativity.

• Manage the change that accompanies growth within your organization.

• Boost productivity and effectiveness.

• Develop communication skills.

• Help your organization attract and retain talented employees.

• Bring work-life balance into the lives of your employees.

• Help your employees thrive.

• Help your company flourish despite uncertain economic times.

"Just four short sessions of meditation training were shown to reduce fatigue and anxiety and significantly improve visuospatial processing, working memory, and decision making."

Zeldon, F., Johnson, S.K., Diamond, B.J., David, Z., & Goolkasian, P., 2010

"Put your wallets back in your pockets. This has nothing to do with money or computers. It's a spiritual shift that needs to take place, not a 'hack'."

Kenau Reeves to Silicon Tech Billionaires

Creating Life Balance

Re-Cap

So, let's recap the ways we've learned to de-stress ourselves:

1. Every experience has a feeling associated with it. Feel it and decide. Make a choice to stay with it or let it go.

2. Listen to yourself. That "gut feeling" is your intuition trying to point you in the right direction.

3. Eat healthy fuel! Choose organic and local offerings, if possible.

4. Consider building your own personal support system. Seek out friends and family members who are positive and healthy. Cultivate these relationships.

5. The act of forgiveness is often overlooked, but it is so incredibly important. Kindly forgive yourself and others for "past" experiences, and the resulting outcomes. How can you move forward if you are focused on things that are no longer relevant? The trick is to live in the NOW. Embrace what is being given to you in the present moment and move gracefully into your future from here.

6. BE grateful, find anything you can be thankful for. At night, before falling asleep, think about the things you are grateful for in your life. Before getting out of bed in the morning, decide to BE grateful for everything that will come to pass on this day.

7. Smile! A smile automatically raises your vibration. You are at the controls!

8. Add more of the key elements to help support your biology, bringing clarity and balance.

9. Explore different forms of meditation and find the ones that works work best for you. (3 X 3)

Pay attention to your intention. Have awareness of awareness. In addition to these recommendations, I highly recommend that you investigate the Resolution Experience. The Resolution Experience is a regression technique that is performed with these specific healing and therapeutic targets as a result. Learn how to heal the cellular memories that are sabotaging your life.

I challenge you to try at least 3 take aways I have shared with you for 2 weeks to start your new lifestyle. Maybe start with increasing your water intake or set aside time to practice the 3-minute meditation. If you noticed your body signaling a magnesium deficiency start, there. We can all use more Oxygen, Water, Magnesium and Movement. This is an opportunity to be a better version of YOU.

This is Susan Davis,
Your expert in Mindfulness & Stress Reduction

Have a great day and keep smiling!

Photo Credit: Julie A. Davis Veach

Take-Away

Frequency & Positive Vibes - BE in Gratitude

EFT - Emotional Freedom Technique

OXYGEN - Breathe
Practice the Ocean Breath
Begin with 3 minutes, 2Xday, &
Building up to 10 minutes 2Xday

MAGNESIUM
Sea Salt/Epsom Salt Soaks
1-2Xday for 20 minutes

WATER - Drink More Water!

MOVEMENT - Love your Body

MEDITATION - Quiet your Mind

Quality Sleep & Relationships

Creating Life Balance

About the Author

My life has been full of diverse experiences, which has led me on a journey of healing and helping others. I feel each person has the potential to be happy and healthy in all aspects of their life, if we just take 'one day at a time,' sometimes one moment at a time. I was adopted at birth by two wonderful parents. My mother was diabetic, and my father was a WWII Veteran who suffered from "shell shock", or PTSD and alcoholism. I married a soldier and have raised three children during a 30-year career in the United States Army.

My military family soon became my extended family; and I sought out ways to help our soldiers returning from war. Many are contemplating suicide and those who don't are living with sleeplessness, hyper vigilance and depression.

From a very young age I had a calling to help others in need. One story that comes to mind is when I was ten years old. I wanted to help "Jerry's kids," referring to the comedian Jerry Lewis, and his efforts to raise awareness for Muscular Dystrophy.

I developed a plan to hold a fair on the tennis court near my home. I created fliers and took them to all of the houses in my community, encouraging attendance on the Saturday of my event. I asked for help from my Girl Scout Troop, inviting my peers to host each of the stations where people could enjoy playing games in exchange for their monetary donations.

I remember playing games like fishing, beanbag toss and darts. It was a very successful event, and I collected over $50! I felt like I had contributed to the well being of others in need, and it felt good.

I have continued to pursue that feeling by tirelessly contributing to all 21 communities where I've lived during a 33-year military career with my husband. Some of those contributions were the CFC, Combined Federal Campaign ($300,000), multiple 501©3 organizations, and time spent raising money for University and College Scholarships for community members.

As a private business owner, I held 6 government contracts for dance and fitness, in both the United States and Europe. Through teaching dance, fitness, yoga and PT (Physical Training) from preschoolers to senior adults I have been able to touch thousands of lives in a positive way, I did this by helping them find specific services needed, experience life changing lessons and discover their passion in life.

I believe we are all spiritual beings having a human experience. I am also becoming increasingly aware of the toxic environment that we are currently living in that is contributing to the stress in our lives, such as preservatives in our food, electromagnetic frequencies (EMF), microwaves and the addictions that sabotage our futures.

Currently, I share my experiences with local Universities and other organizations, on the topics of Self-Empowerment and Stress Reduction.

While living in Hawaii, I taught reintegration courses through the Department of Defense to our returning soldiers from Operation Enduring Freedom, and Operation Iraqi Freedom, along with their families. Some of the topics I covered in these reintegration workshops were Stress on and Off the Battlefield, Deployment Reunion for Couples, Home with the Kids workshops, Anger Management, Single with Children Readiness, Single Soldier Reintegration, Money Management and Divorce Recovery Workshops.

One of my community projects was a 30-minute video documentary "You Are Not Alone-Unveiling the self-violence and suicidal tendencies among Gay, Bisexual, Lesbian, Transgender and Questioning Youth", based on the real and personal stories within the LGTBQ community. I presented this at the Suicide Prevention Regional Conference in Fort Collins, Colorado.

I was a guest speaker at Bethune-Cookman University, in Daytona Beach, Florida. My speech was directed towards the women attending the "Powerful Women Collaborating" seminars. I have realized from an early age that some of the greatest rewards in life are found in helping others, while expecting nothing in return. Ironically, these efforts tend to come back to me in so many varied and wonderful ways.

I have been a guest speaker for the American Society on Aging National Convention, the Performance Coach behind the scenes of "Girl Starter", an entrepreneurial reality TV show about girls ages 18-23 on TLC, The Girls in Tech Global Conference, in San Francisco, California and The Pioneers Conference in Vienna, Austria.

I earned a graduate degree in Energy Medicine/ Transpersonal Psychology and am an Integrative Health/Life Coach for the US Olympic Figure Skating team, many other professional athletes, as well as for Corporate Executives across the United States. I have an extensive leadership background focusing on implementation and evaluation of programs related to quality of life and recreation for the Department of Defense, I developed stress reduction techniques with the US Army, and worked with them for over 20 years. Using my spiritual background, I have integrated stress reduction techniques into my Healing Yoga Classes and have also practiced these with returning Soldiers. I am a practicing Reiki Master and co-

Photo Credit: Collete Davis

author of "War Time Coping Strategies".
I am grateful for all of my experiences. My diverse experiences in life have helped me be a more compassionate observer, willing to meet and assist others where they are currently. As a performance coach, I have helped enhance each individual to increase their quality of life and optimal performance. This book has been written to help you discover where your stressors reside. With this knowledge you can utilize the simple practices and strategies to reduce and eliminate your stress.

We invite you to join Susan on her socials:

 SusanPerformance

 SusanPerformanc

 SusanPerformanceCoach

 SusanPerformance

Join the Group!

"Susan Wellness News"
Susan's official newsletter for wellness tips & news

www.SusanPerformance.com/WellnessNews

Bibliography

Ballentine, Rudolph, M.D. Radical Healing: Integrating the World's Great Therapeutic Traditions to Create a New Transformative Medicine. New York, NY: Three Rivers Press, 1999.

Bland, J. (2017). Defining function in the functional medicine model. Integrative Medicine: A Clinician's Journal, 16(1), 22-25. Retrieved from https://www.ncbi. nlm.nih.gov/pmc/articles/PMC5312741/

Boon, H.S., Ng, J.Y., Thompson, A.K., & Whitehead, C.R. (2016). Making sense of "alternative", "complementary", "unconventional" and "integrative" medicine: Exploring the terms and meanings through a textual analysis. BMC Complementary and Alternative Medicine, 16(1), 134. Retrieved from https:// bmccomplementalternmed.biomedcentral.com/articles/10.1186/s12906-015-0696-2

Braden, Gregg. Resilience from the Heart - The Power to Thrive in Life's Extremes. New York, NY: Hayhouse Publishers, 2015.

Branson, Richard. Finding My Virginity. New York, NY: Penguin Random House, 2017.

Brewer, Allexia. Monadiki - The Goddess of Fierce Leadership, Purposely Created Publishing Group, 2017.

Carter, Karen Rauch. Move Your Stuff Change Your Life - How to Use Feng Shui to Get Love, Money, Respect, and Happiness. New York, NY: Fireside, 2000.

Church, Dawson. The Genie in Your Genes. Santa Rosa, CA: Energy Psychology Press., 2014.

Condron, Daniel R. Dreams of the Soul: The Yogi Sutras of Patanjali. Windyville, MO: SOM Publishing, 1999.

Craig, Gary. The EFT Manual, Santa Rosa, CA: Energy Psychology Press, 2008.

Doidge, Norman. The Brain That Changes Itself - Stories of Personal Triumph from the Frontiers of Brain Science. New York, NY: Penguin Publishing, 2007.

Donovan, Sean., Kevin Snyder. The Bookbook - A Recipe for Writing and Publishing Your Book: CreateSpace, 2015.

Emoto, Marsaru. The Hidden Messages in Water. New York, NY: Atria Books, 2004.

Favilli, Elena., Cavallo, Francesca. Good Night Stories for Rebel Girls - 100 Tales of Extraordinary Women. India: Penguin Random House, 2016.

Gates, Rolf, Kenison, Katrina. Meditations from the Mat - Daily Reflections on the Path of Yoga. New York, NY: Anchor, 2002.

Gundry, Steve R. The Plant Paradox: The Hidden Dangers in "Healthy" Foods

That Cause Disease and Weight Gain. New York, New York: Harper Collins, 2017.

Haidt, Jonathan. The Happiness Hypothesis - Finding Modern Truth in Ancient Wisdom. New York, NY: Basic Books, 2006.

Hartley, Scott. The Fuzzy and the Techie - Why Liberal Arts Will Rule the Digital World. New York, NY: Houghton Mifflin Harcourt Publishing Company, 2017.

Hartwig, Melissa., Hartwig, Dallas. The Whole 30 - The 30-Day Guide to Total Health and Food Freedom. New York, NY: Houghton Mifflin Harcourt Publishing Company, 2015.

Hauser, Fran. The Myth of the Nice Girl – Achieving a Career You Love Without Becoming a Person You Hate, New York, NY: Houghton Mifflin Harcourt, 2018.

Henrich, Joseph. The Secret of Our Success - How Culture is Driving Human Evolution Domesticating Our Species and Making Us Smarter. Princeton, NJ, 2016.

Hirschi, Gertrud. Mudras - Yoga in Your Hands. Newburyport, MA: Weiser Books, 2016.

Huber, Regina. Speak Up, Stand Out and Shine - Speak Powerfully in Any Situation.

Johnson, Chris & Matt. Capacity - Create Laser Focus, Boundless Energy, and an Unstoppable Drive in Any Organization. Hoboken, NJ: John Wiley & Sons, Inc. 2018.

Lipton, Bruce H. Biology of Belief: Unleashing the Power of Consciousness, Matter and Miracles. Santa Rosa, CA: Mountain of Love/Elite Books, 2005.

Marciocia, Giovanni. The Foundations of Chinese Medicine. New York, NY: Churchill Livingston, Inc., 1989.

McTaggert, Lynne. The Field: The Quest for the Secret Force of the Universe. New York, NY: Harper Collins, 2002.

O"Dea, James. Cultivating Peace - Becoming a 21st Century Peace Ambassador. San Rafael, CA: Shift Books, 2012.

O'Dea, James. The Conscious Activist- Where Activism Meets Mysticism. Watkins,

Pacholok, Sally M., Stuart, Jeffrey J. Could it Be B12 - An Epidemic of Misdiagnoses. Fresno, CA: Quill Driver Books, 2006.

Patrick, Danica. Pretty Intense - The 90-Day Mind, Body and Food Plan that will absolutely Change Your Life. New York, NY: Penguin Random House, 2017.

Perlmutter, David. Brain Maker - The Power of Gut Microbes to Heal and

Protect Your Brain-for Life. New York, NY: Little, Brown Company, 2015.

Pert, Candace B. Molecules of Emotion: The Scientific Basis. Edinburgh, UK: Harcourt Publishers, 2000.

Proctor, Dina. Madly Chasing Peace - How I Went from Hell to Happy in Nine Minutes a Day. New York, NY: Morgan James Publishing, 2013.

Pham, Tiffany. You Are A Mogul – How to Do the Impossible Do it Yourself & Do it Now, New York, NY: Simon & Schuster, 2018.

Radin, Dean. Entangled Minds/ Extrasensory Experiences in a Quantum Reality. New York, NY: Pocket Books/Simon & Schuster, Inc., 2006.

Rauch Carter, Karen. Move Your Stuff, Change Your Life. New York, New York: Simon & Schuster, Inc., 2000.

Ruiz, Don Miguel. The Four Agreements. San Rafael, CA: Amber-Allen Publishing, Inc., 1997.

Schlotterbeck, Karl. Living Your Past Lives: The Psychology of Past-Life Regression. New York, NY: Ballantine Books, 1987.

Shealy, C. Norman. Energy Medicine. Virginia Beach, VA: 4th Dimension Press, 2016.

Shealy, C. Norman. Life Beyond 100 - Secrets of the Fountain of Youth. New York, NY: Penguin Group, 2005.

Sinek, Simon. Leaders Eat Last. New York, NY: Penguin Random House, 2017.

Sobel, Dava. The Glass Universe - How Ladies of the Harvard Observatory Took the Measure of the Stars. New York, NY: Viking, 2016.

Strom, Max. There is No APP for Happiness - How to Avoid a Near-Life Experience. New York, NY: Skyhorse Publishing, 2013.

Summers, Marshall Vian. Life in The Universe - The Reality and Spirituality. Boulder, CO: The Society for the New Message, 2012.

Tenzin-Dolma, Lisa. Healing Mandalas - 30 Inspiring Meditations to Soothe Your Mind, Body & Soul. New York, NY: Sterling Publishing Company, 2008.

Thieriot, Elisabeth. Be Fabulous at Any Age - Creating Ageless Skin Through Seasonal Living. San Francisco, CA: 2011.

Made in the USA
Columbia, SC
18 January 2021